HMH

Assessment Readiness

and Practice Tests

Grade 4

Includes:

- Benchmark Tests
- Performance Assessment Tasks
- Test Taking Strategies
- Targeted Practice of Concepts and Skills

Printed in the U.S.A.

ISBN 978-1-328-51918-4

1 2 3 4 5 6 7 8 9 10 0607 30 29 28 27 26 25

4500924619 B C D E F G

Contents

Assessment Formats

Many of today's mathematics assessments contain item types beyond the traditional multiple-choice format, which allows for a more robust assessment of students' understanding of concepts.

Many of these mathematics assessments will be administered via computers, and *Assessment Readiness and Practice Tests* presents items in formats similar to what you will see on the tests. The following information is provided to help familiarize you with these different types of items. Each item type is identified on pages (vii–viii). The examples will introduce you to the item types.

The following explanations are provided to guide you in answering the questions. These pages (v–vi) describe the most common item types. You may find other types on some tests.

Example 1 Identify examples of a property.

More Than One Correct Choice

This type of item looks like a traditional multiple-choice item, but it asks you to mark all that apply. To mark all that apply, look for more than one correct choice. Carefully look at each choice and mark it if it is a correct answer.

Example 2 Circle the word that completes the sentence.

Choose From a List

Sometimes when you take a test on a computer, you will have to select a word, number, or symbol from a drop-down list. The *Assessment Readiness and Practice Tests* practice tests and worksheets show a list and ask you to choose the correct answer. Make your choice by circling the correct answer. There will only be one choice that is correct.

Example 3 Sort numbers by even or odd.

Sorting

You may be asked to sort something into categories. These items will present numbers, words, or equations on rectangular "tiles." The directions will ask you to write each of the items in the box that describes it.

When the sorting involves more complex equations or drawings, each tile will have a letter next to it. You will be asked to write the letter for the tile in the box. Sometimes you may write the same number or word in more than one box. For example, if you need to sort quadrilaterals by category, a square could be in a box labeled *rectangle* and another box labeled *rhombus*.

Example 4 Order numbers from least to greatest.

Use Given Numbers in the Answer

You may also see numbers and symbols on tiles when you are asked to write an equation or answer a question using only numbers. You should use the given numbers to write the answer to the problem. Sometimes there will be extra numbers. You may also need to use each number more than once.

Example 5 Match related facts.

Matching

Some items will ask you to match equivalent values or other related items. The directions will specify what you should match. There will be dots to guide you in drawing lines. The matching may be between columns or rows.

Item Types:

Example 1

More Than One Correct Choice

Fill in the bubble next to all the correct answers.

Select the equations that show the Commutative Property of Addition. Mark all that apply.

Ⓐ $35 + 56 = 30 + 5 + 50 + 6$

Ⓑ $47 + 68 = 68 + 47$

Ⓒ $32 + 54 = 54 + 32$

Ⓓ $12 + 90 = 90 + 12$

Ⓔ $346 + 932 = 900 + 346 + 32$

Ⓕ $45 + 167 = 40 + 167 + 5$

Example 2

Choose From a List

Circle the word that completes the sentence.

$(25 + 17) + 23 = 25 + (17 + 23)$

The equation shows the addends in a different

order.
grouping.
operation.

Example 3

Sorting

Copy the numbers in the correct box.

Write each number in the box below the word that describes it.

33 46 72 97

Even	Odd

Example 4

Use Given Numbers in the Answer

Write the given numbers to answer the question.

Write the numbers in order from least to greatest.

345 267 390 714 873

_____ _____ _____ _____ _____

Example 5

Matching

Draw lines to match an item in one column to the related item in the other column.

Match the pairs of related facts.

$8 + 7 = 15$ •	• $12 - 9 = 3$
$14 - 8 = 6$ •	• $7 + 8 = 15$
$3 + 9 = 12$ •	• $9 + 7 = 16$
$16 - 7 = 9$ •	• $14 - 6 = 8$

Name ______________________________

Practice Test

Learning Objective
Interpret a multiplication equation as a comparison and a multiplicative comparison as an equation.

1. For numbers 1a–1c, write an equation or a comparison sentence using the numbers on the tiles.

3	4	6	8	8
9	27	32	48	

1a.

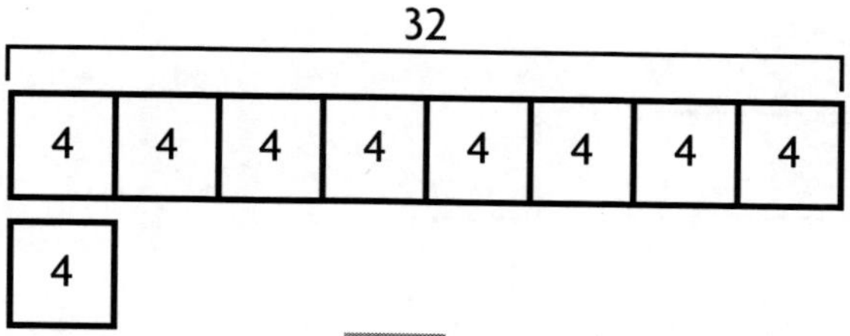

☐ times as many as ☐ is ☐.

1b.

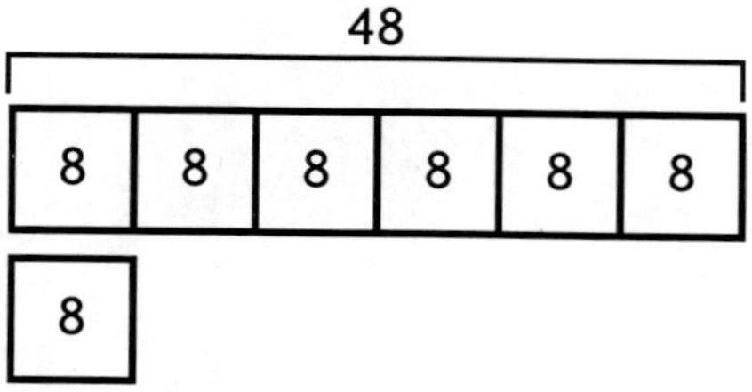

☐ × ☐ = ☐

1c. $9 \times 3 = 27$

☐ times as many as ☐ is ☐.

2. For numbers 2a–2b, write an equation or a comparison sentence using the numbers on the tiles.

3	4	7
9	21	36

2a.

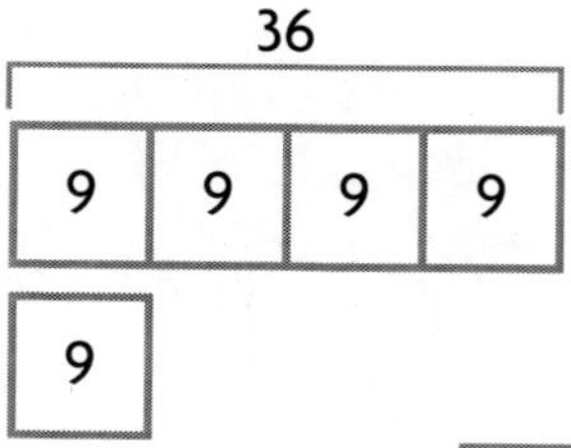

☐ times as many as ☐ is ☐.

2b.

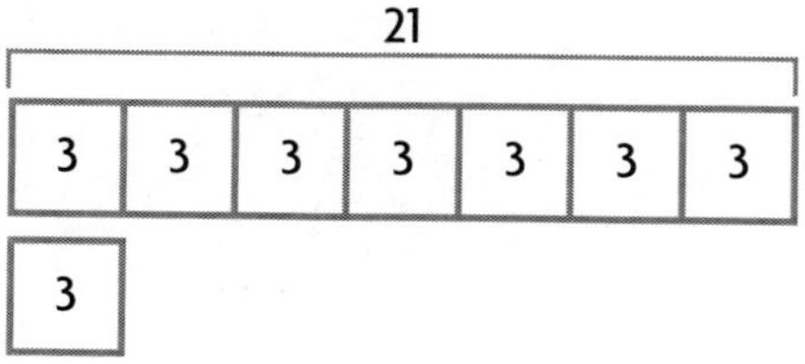

☐ × ☐ = ☐

GO ON

Name ___________________________

3. At the pet fair, Darlene's dog weighed 5 times as much as Leah's dog. Together, the dogs weighed 84 pounds. How much did each dog weigh? Complete the bar model. Write an equation and solve.

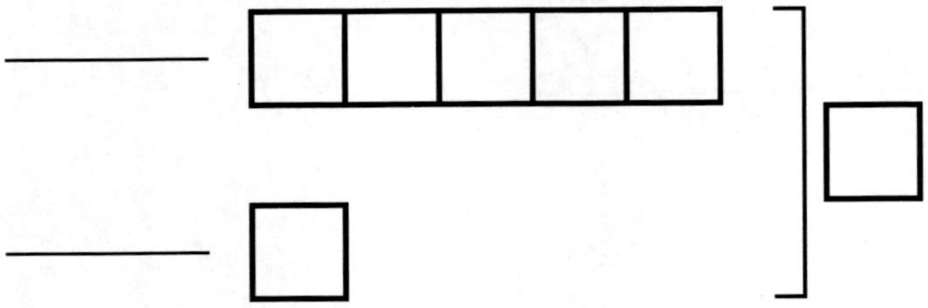

4. Heidi's mom made flower arrangements for a party. She made 4 times as many rose arrangements as tulip arrangements. Heidi's mom made a total of 40 arrangements. How many flower arrangements of each type did Heidi's mom make? Complete the bar model. Write an equation and solve.

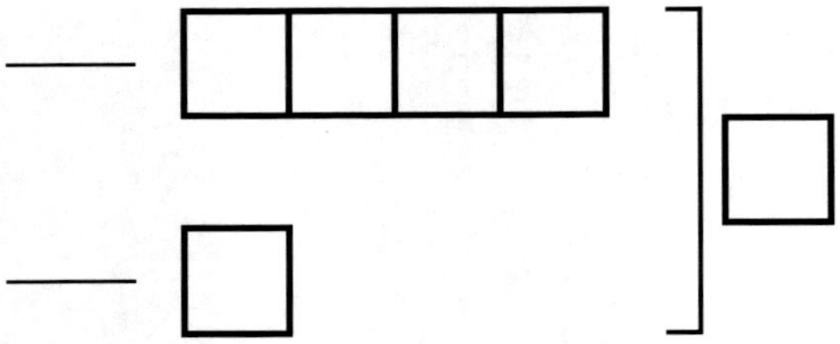

STOP

Name ______________________________

Practice Test

Learning Objective
Solve word problems with whole numbers involving multiplicative comparison distinguishing between multiplicative and additive comparisons.

1. Ursula bought 9 dozen rolls of first-aid tape for the health office. The rolls were divided equally into 4 boxes. How many rolls are in each box?

_______ rolls

2. There are 112 seats in the school auditorium. There are 7 seats in each row. There are 70 people seated, filling up full rows of seats. How many rows are empty?

_______ rows

3. Last weekend, Mandy collected 4 times as many shells as Cameron. Together, they collected 40 shells. How many shells did Mandy collect? Write an equation and solve.

Mandy collected _______ shells.

4. The soccer team sells 72 bagels with cream cheese for $2 each during a bake sale. The coach wants to use the bake sale money to buy socks for the 14 players at $6 a pair. If the coach spends all of the money on socks, how many extra pairs of socks will he have? Explain how you found your answer.

____

____

____

____

____

____

____

____

GO ON

Name ___

5. Chad bought 8 dozen note pads for his office. The note pads were divided equally into 6 boxes. How many note pads are in each box?

_____ note pads

6. There are 126 seats in a meeting room. There are 9 seats in each row. There are 90 people seated, filling up full rows of seats. How many rows are empty?

_____ rows

7. The number of gray pigeons on a wire is 6 times the number of white pigeons. Choose one expression from each column to create an equation that compares the number of gray pigeons (g) and white pigeons (w).

○ $g \div 6$		○ $w - 6$
○ $6g$	=	○ $6w$
○ g		○ $w + 5$
○ $g - 6$		○ w

8. The number of ash trees on a tree farm is 5 times the number of pine trees. Choose one expression from each column to create an equation that compares the number of ash trees (a) and pine trees (p).

○ $a - 5$		○ p
○ $5a$	=	○ $5p$
○ a		○ $p + 5$
○ $a \div 5$		○ $p - 5$

STOP

Name ______________________________

Practice Test

Learning Objective
Solve word problems with multi-digit whole numbers using the four operations, including problems in which a remainder is interpreted.

1. Rudy will buy 3 ivory silk lilac trees or 2 bur oak trees. He wants to buy the trees that cost less. What trees will he buy? How much will he save? Show your work.

Prices for Trees					
Tree	**Regular Price**	**Price for 3 or more**	**Tree**	**Regular Price**	**Price for 3 or more**
Ivory Silk Lilac	\$25	\$22	Hazelnut	\$9	\$8
White Pine	\$25	\$37	Red Maple	\$9	\$8
Bur Oak	\$35	\$32	Birch	\$9	\$8

2. There are 3 new seats in each row in a school auditorium. There are 15 rows in the auditorium. Each new seat costs \$74. What is the cost for the new seats? Explain how you found your answer.

3. Nolan divides his 88 toy cars into boxes. Each box holds 9 cars. How many boxes does Nolan need to store all of his cars?

________ boxes

GO ON

Name ___________________________

4. Kris and Julio played a card game. Together, they scored 36 points in one game. Kris scored 2 times as many points as Julio. How many points did Kris and Julio each score? Write an equation and solve. Explain your work.

5. A kennel is moving 160 dogs to a new facility. Each dog has its own crate. The facility manager rents 17 trucks. Each truck holds 9 dogs in their crates.

Part A

Write a division problem that can be used to find the number of trucks needed to carry the dogs in their crates. Then solve.

Part B

What does the remainder mean in the context of the problem?

Part C

How can you use your answer to determine if the facility manager rented enough trucks? Explain.

STOP

Name ______________________________

Practice Test

Learning Objective
Find all factor pairs for a whole number in the range 1–100, and recognize that a whole number is a multiple of its factors. Determine whether a given whole number is prime or composite.

1. List all the factor pairs in the table.

Factors of 48	
____ × ____ = ____	____, ____
____ × ____ = ____	____, ____
____ × ____ = ____	____, ____
____ × ____ = ____	____, ____
____ × ____ = ____	____, ____

2. Brady has a card collection with 64 basketball cards, 32 football cards, and 24 baseball cards. He wants to arrange the cards in equal piles, with only one type of card in each pile. How many cards can he put in each pile? Mark all that apply.

Ⓐ 1 Ⓑ 2 Ⓒ 3 Ⓓ 4 Ⓔ 8 Ⓕ 32

3. Manny makes dinner using 1 box of pasta and 1 jar of sauce. If pasta is sold in packages of 6 boxes and sauce is sold in packages of 3 jars, what is the least number of dinners that Manny can make without any supplies left over?

________ dinners

4. Marissa was decorating her room. She arranged 63 same-size picture tiles on a wall in the shape of a rectangle. Which are possible arrangements of the picture tiles? Mark all that apply.

Ⓐ 7 rows of 9 tiles

Ⓑ 22 rows of 6 tiles

Ⓒ 21 rows of 3 tiles

Ⓓ 63 rows of 1 tile

Ⓔ 32 rows of 2 tiles

GO ON

Name ___________________________________

5. Eric had 13 tiles to arrange in a rectangular design. He drew a model of the rectangles he could make with the 13 tiles.

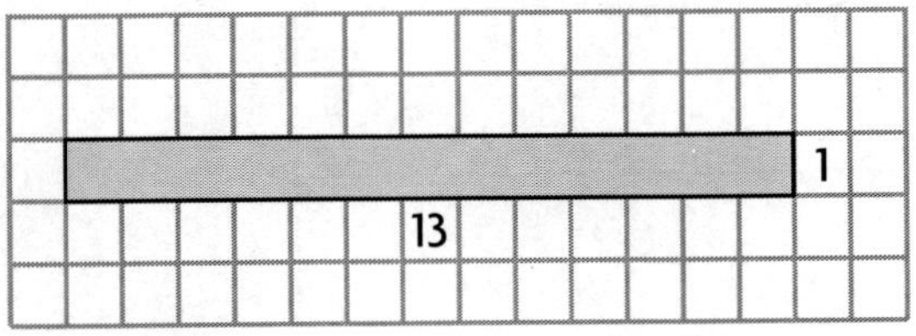

Part A

How does Eric's drawing show that 13 is a prime number?

Part B

Suppose Eric used 12 tiles to make the rectangular design. How many different rectangles could he make with the 12 tiles? Write a list or draw a picture to show the number and dimensions of the rectangles he could make.

Part C

Eric's friend Dawn said that she could make a larger number of different designs with 15 tiles than with Eric's 13 tiles. Do you agree with Dawn? Explain.

STOP

Name ______________________________

Practice Test

Learning Objective
Generate a shape or number pattern that follows a given rule.

1. Jill wrote the number 40. If her rule is *add 7*, what is the fourth number in Jill's pattern? How can you check your answer?

2. Erica knits 18 squares on Monday. She knits 7 more squares each day from Tuesday through Friday. How many squares does Erica have in all by the end of the day on Friday?

______ squares

3. Use the rule to write the first five terms of the pattern.

Rule: Add 10, subtract 5 First term: 11

____

4. Jose wrote the number 36. If his rule is *add 6*, what is the fourth number in Jose's pattern? How can you check your answer?

5. Aidan makes 12 bracelets on Monday. He makes 8 more bracelets each day from Tuesday through Friday. How many bracelets does Aidan have in all by the end of the day on Friday?

______ bracelets

GO ON

Name ______________________________

6. Use the rule to write the first five terms of the pattern.

Rule: Add 8, subtract 4 First term: 13

____

7. Use the rule to find the next 3 terms in the pattern.

Rule: multiply by 2

4, 8, 16, 32, ☐, ☐, ☐

8. Draw the next term of the pattern.

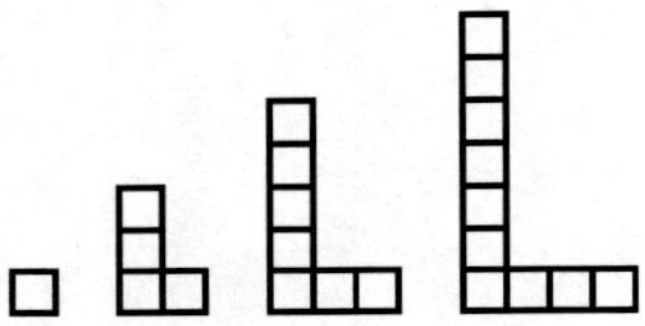

9. Use the rule to find the next 3 terms in the pattern.

Rule: multiply by 3

3, 9, 27, 81, ☐, ☐, ☐, ...

10. Draw the next term of the pattern.

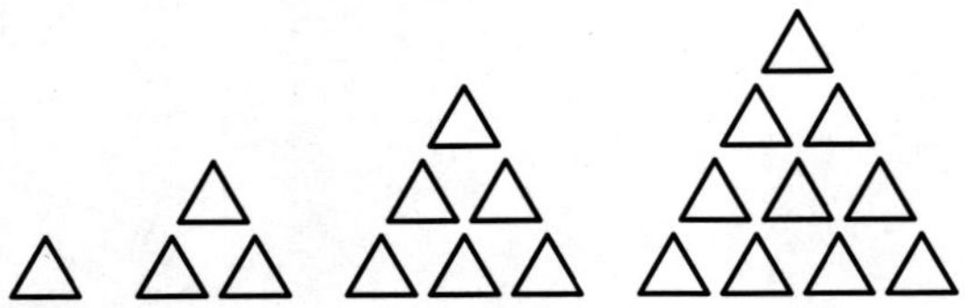

STOP

Name ____________________

Practice Test

Learning Objective
Show that a digit in one place represents ten times what it represents in the place to its right.

1. Nancy wrote the greatest number that can be made using each of these digits exactly once.

5	3	4	9	8	1

Part A

What was Nancy's number? How do you know this is the greatest possible number for these digits?

Part B

What is the least number that can be made using each digit exactly once? Explain why the value of the 4 is greater than the value of the 5.

2. Circle the choice that completes the statement.

10,000 less than 24,576 is [equal to / greater than / less than] 1,000 less than 14,576.

3. Caden made a four-digit number with a 5 in the thousands place, a 5 in the ones place, a 6 in the tens place, and a 4 in the hundreds place. What was the number?

____

GO ON

Name ___________________________

4. Leslie wrote the greatest number that can be made using each of these digits exactly once.

6	2	4	7	9	1

Part A

What was Leslie's number? How do you know this is the greatest possible number for these digits?

Part B

What is the least number that can be made using each digit exactly once? Explain why the value of the 4 is greater than the value of the 6.

5. Which statements are true? Mark all that apply.

Ⓐ The value of 2 in 724,638 is 20,000.

Ⓑ The value of 8 in 380,194 is 800,000.

Ⓒ The value of 7 in 671,235 is 70,000.

Ⓓ The value of 9 in 874,092 is 900.

6. Carson made a four-digit number with a 4 in the thousands place, a 4 in the ones place, a 5 in the tens place, and a 6 in the hundreds place. What was the number?

____

STOP

Name ______________________________

Practice Test

Learning Objective
Use word form, standard form, and expanded form to read, write, and represent whole numbers to 1,000,000.

1. Write the name of each mountain peak in the box that describes its height, in feet.

U.S. Mountain Peaks					
Name	**State**	**Height (ft)**	**Name**	**State**	**Height (ft)**
Blanca Peak	CO	14,345	Mount Whitney	CA	14,494
Crestone Peak	CO	14,294	University Peak	AK	14,470
Humboldt Peak	CO	14,064	White Mountain	CA	14,246

Between 14,000 feet and 14,300 feet	Between 14,301 feet and 14,500 feet

2. Select another way to show 403,871. Mark all that apply.

Ⓐ four hundred three thousand, eight hundred one

Ⓑ four hundred three thousand, seventy-one

Ⓒ four hundred three thousand, eight hundred seventy-one

Ⓓ 400,000 + 38,000 + 800 + 70 + 1

Ⓔ 400,000 + 3,000 + 800 + 70 + 1

Ⓕ 4 hundred thousands + 3 thousands + 8 hundreds + 7 tens + 1 one

3. A college baseball team had 3 games in April. Game one had an attendance of 14,753 people. Game two had an attendance of 20,320 people. Game three had an attendance of 14,505 people. Write the games in order from the least attendance to the greatest attendance. Use pictures, words, or numbers to show how you know.

GO ON

Name ______________________________

4 Select a number for ☐ that will make a true comparison. Mark all that apply.

807,058 > ☐

- Ⓐ 870,508
- Ⓑ 870,058
- Ⓒ 807,508
- Ⓓ 807,085
- Ⓔ 805,058
- Ⓕ 800,758

5. Select another way to show 106,423. Mark all that apply.

- Ⓐ 100,000 + 6,000 + 400 + 20 + 3
- Ⓑ 1 hundred thousand + 6 thousands + 4 hundreds + 2 tens + 3 ones
- Ⓒ one hundred six thousand, twenty-three
- Ⓓ 100,000 + 16,000 + 400 + 20 + 3
- Ⓔ one hundred six thousand, four hundred three
- Ⓕ one hundred six thousand, four hundred twenty-three

6. Match the number to the value of its 5.

36,458 •	• 5
375,123 •	• 50
18,005 •	• 50,000
52,789 •	• 5,000

7. An ice-skating competition lasted three days. Day one had an attendance of 16,390 people. Day two had an attendance of 16,550 people. Day three had an attendance of 16,237 people. Write the days in order from least attendance to greatest attendance. Use pictures, words, or numbers to show how you know.

STOP

Name ______________________________

Practice Test

Learning Objective
Round multi-digit whole numbers to a given place value.

1. Bobby and Cheryl each rounded 745,829 to the nearest ten thousand. Bobby wrote 750,000, and Cheryl wrote 740,000. Who is correct? Explain the error that was made.

2. The total season attendance for a college team's home games, rounded to the nearest ten thousand, was 270,000. Which number could be the exact attendance?

   Ⓐ 265,888

   Ⓑ 260,987

   Ⓒ 276,499

   Ⓓ 206,636

3. There were 13,501 visitors to a museum in June. What is this number rounded to the nearest ten thousand? Explain how you rounded.

   ____

   ____

4. The total season attendance for a professional football team's home games, rounded to the nearest ten thousand, was 710,000. Could 701,752 be the exact attendance for the season? Explain your answer.

GO ON

Name ______________________________

5. Luis and Liz each rounded 635,974 to the nearest ten thousand. Luis wrote 630,000, and Liz wrote 640,000. Who is correct? Explain the error that was made.

6. There were 12,351 visitors to a history center last year. What is this number rounded to the nearest hundred? Explain how you rounded.

7. The number of people who attended a festival, rounded to the nearest hundred thousand, was 300,000. Which could be the exact number of people who attended the festival?

- (A) 351,213
- (B) 249,899
- (C) 252,348
- (D) 389,001

STOP

Name ____

Practice Test
Learning Objective
Add and subtract multi-digit whole numbers using a standard algorithmic approach.

For numbers 1–2, use the table.

Population of Sacramento, CA			
Age in years	**Population**	**Age in years**	**Population**
Under 5	35,010	20 to 34	115,279
5 to 9	31,406	35 to 49	92,630
10 to 14	30,253	50 to 64	79,271
15 to 19	34,219	65 and over	49,420

1. How many children are under 10 years old? Show your work.

2. How many people are between the ages of 20 and 49? Show your work.

3. New Mexico has an area of 121,298 square miles. California has an area of 155,779 square miles. How much greater is the area, in square miles, of California than the area of New Mexico? Show your work and explain how you know the answer is reasonable.

GO ON

Name ___________________________

For numbers 4–5, use the table.

Population of Fresno, CA			
Age in years	**Population**	**Age in years**	**Population**
Under 5	43,911	20 to 34	119,388
5 to 9	40,087	35 to 49	89,416
10 to 14	39,634	50 to 64	72,261
15 to 19	43,867	65 and over	46,101

4. How many people are between the ages of 35 and 64? Show your work.

5. How many more children are under the age of 5 than between the ages of 10 and 14? Show your work.

6. Arizona has a land area of 113,998 square miles. Wyoming has a land area of 97,813 square miles. How much greater is the area, in square miles, of Arizona than the area of Wyoming? Show your work and explain how you know the answer is reasonable.

STOP

Practice Test

Learning Objective
Multiply a whole number of up to four digits by a one-digit whole number or multiply two two-digit numbers using place value understanding and properties of operations.

Name ______________________________

1. Part A

Draw a line to match each section in the model to the partial product it represents.

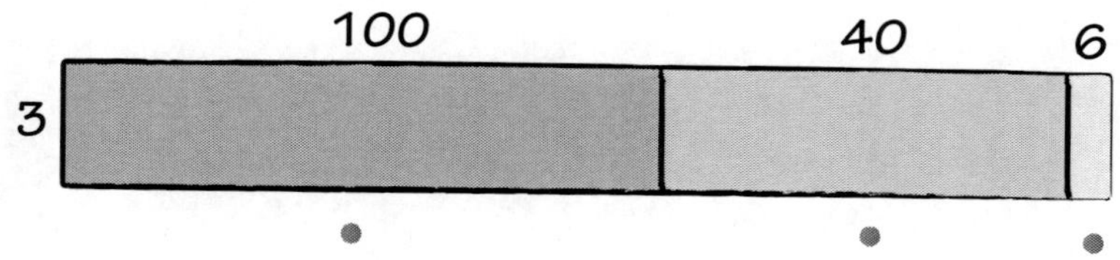

3×6 $\qquad$ 3×100 $\qquad$ 3×40

Part B

Then find 3×146. Show your work and explain.

2. It costs 9,328 points to build each apartment building in the computer game Big City Building. What is the cost to build 5 apartment buildings? Show your work.

GO ON

Name ______________________________

3. Write the unknown digits. Use each digit exactly once.

```
     51
 ×   28
 ------
  1,□00
    □00
     □0
 +    □
 ------
  □,428
```

1	2	4	8	0

4. Write the unknown digits. Use each digit exactly once.

```
     46
 ×   93
 ------
  3,□00
    5□0
    □20
 +   1□
 ------
  4,□78
```

1	2	4	6	8

5. Julius and Walt are finding the product of 25 and 16.

Julius

```
    25
 ×  16
 -----
   250
 + 150
 -----
   500
```

Walt

```
    25
 ×  16
 -----
   200
   120
   300
 +  50
 -----
   670
```

Part A

Both answers are incorrect. What did Julius do wrong? What did Walt do wrong?

Part B

What is the correct product?

STOP

Name ______________________________

Practice Test

Learning Objective
Divide whole numbers with up to four-digit dividends and one-digit divisors using place value understanding, properties of operations, and/or the relationship between multiplication and division.

1. Which quotients are equal to 300? Mark all that apply.

   Ⓐ 1,200 ÷ 4   Ⓒ 2,400 ÷ 8   Ⓔ 9,000 ÷ 3

   Ⓑ 180 ÷ 9   Ⓓ 2,100 ÷ 7   Ⓕ 3,000 ÷ 3

2. A traveling circus brings along everything it needs for its shows in big trucks.

   Part A

   The circus sets up chairs in rows with 9 seats in each row. How many rows will need to be set up if 513 people are expected to attend the show?

   ________ rows

   Part B

   Can the rows be divided into a number of equal sections? Explain how you found your answer.

   Part C

   Circus horses eat about 250 pounds of horse food per week. About how many pounds of food does a circus horse eat each day? Explain.

GO ON

Name ______________________________

3. Which division sentence has a quotient with a remainder?

Ⓐ 320 ÷ 4

Ⓑ 420 ÷ 3

Ⓒ 650 ÷ 4

Ⓓ 360 ÷ 9

4. Which quotients are equal to 20? Mark all that apply.

Ⓐ 120 ÷ 4

Ⓑ 180 ÷ 9

Ⓒ 120 ÷ 6

Ⓓ 180 ÷ 6

5. Use partial quotients. Fill in the blanks.

$$\begin{array}{r} 7\overline{)749} \\ -\boxed{} \\ \hline \boxed{} \\ -\boxed{} \\ \hline \boxed{} \end{array} \qquad \begin{array}{rr} 100 \times 7 & \boxed{} \\ 7 \times 7 & +\boxed{} \\ \hline & \boxed{} \end{array}$$

STOP

Name ____________________

Practice Test

Learning Objective
Explain why a fraction, *a/b*, is equivalent to a fraction $(n \times a)/(n \times b)$ using visual fraction models.

1. For numbers 1a–1d, tell whether the fractions are equivalent by selecting the correct symbol.

1a. $\frac{3}{12}$ [= / ≠] $\frac{1}{4}$

1b. $\frac{3}{5}$ [= / ≠] $\frac{9}{10}$

1c. $\frac{5}{6}$ [= / ≠] $\frac{10}{12}$

1d. $\frac{6}{10}$ [= / ≠] $\frac{5}{8}$

2. In the school chorus, $\frac{2}{12}$ of the students are fourth graders. In simplest form, what fraction of the students in the school chorus are fourth graders?

__________ of the students

3. Frank has two same-size rectangles divided into the same number of equal parts. One rectangle has $\frac{3}{4}$ of the parts shaded, and the other has $\frac{1}{3}$ of the parts shaded.

Into how many parts could each rectangle be divided? Show your work by drawing the parts of each rectangle and shading the correct amounts.

4. Fill in the missing numerators to make chains of equivalent fractions.

$\frac{1}{2} = \frac{\square}{10} = \frac{\square}{100}$

$\frac{2}{3} = \frac{\square}{9} = \frac{\square}{12}$

$\frac{3}{4} = \frac{\square}{8} = \frac{\square}{100}$

GO ON

Name ______________________________

5. Morita works in a florist shop and makes flower arrangements in vases. She puts 10 flowers in each vase, and $\frac{2}{10}$ of the flowers are daisies.

Part A

If Morita makes 10 arrangements, how many daisies does she need? Show how you can check your answer.

_______ daisies

6. Geoff is making gift bags for his friends. There are stickers in $\frac{1}{4}$ of the gift bags. If Geoff makes 12 gift bags, how many will contain stickers?

_______ gift bags

7. Craig is tiling the floor of his bathroom. He wants $\frac{1}{4}$ of the tiles to be brown. What other fractions can represent the part of the tiles that will be brown? Shade the models to show your work.

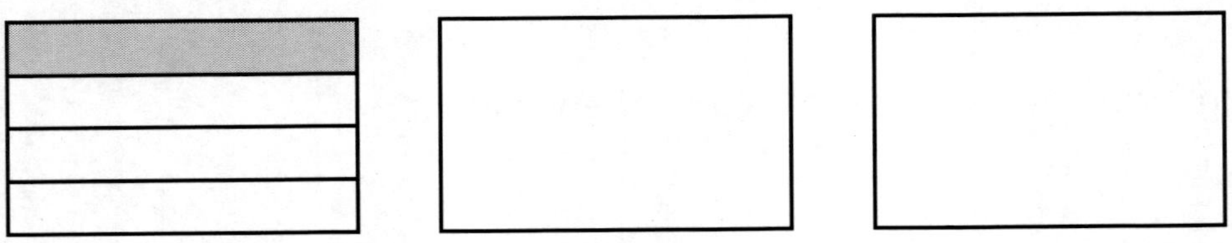

$\frac{1}{4}$ $\frac{\square}{8}$ $\frac{\square}{\square}$

STOP

Name ______________________________

Practice Test

Learning Objective
Compare fractions with different numerators and different denominators using $<$, $>$, or $=$, recognizing that the comparisons are only valid when the fractions refer to the same whole.

1. Juan's mother gave him a recipe for trail mix.

$\frac{3}{4}$ cup cereal	$\frac{2}{3}$ cup almonds
$\frac{1}{4}$ cup peanuts	$\frac{1}{2}$ cup raisins

Order the ingredients used in the recipe from least to greatest.

2. Darcy bought $\frac{1}{2}$ pound of cheese and $\frac{3}{4}$ pound of hamburger for a barbecue. Use the numbers to compare the amounts of cheese and hamburger Darcy bought.

$$\frac{\square}{\square} < \frac{\square}{\square}$$

1	3
2	4

3. Suki rode her bike $\frac{4}{5}$ mile. Claire rode her bike $\frac{1}{3}$ mile. They want to compare how far they each rode their bikes.

Suki rode her bike [a longer distance than / the same distance as / a shorter distance than] Claire.

4. Theo has $\frac{2}{3}$ yard of blue fabric and $\frac{3}{4}$ yard of red fabric. He wants to compare the amounts of blue and red fabric he has.

$\frac{2}{3}$ [$<$ / $>$ / $=$] $\frac{3}{4}$

GO ON

Name ______________________________

5. Regina, Courtney, and Ellen hiked around Bear Pond. Regina hiked $\frac{7}{10}$ of the distance in an hour. Courtney hiked $\frac{3}{6}$ of the distance in an hour. Ellen hiked $\frac{3}{8}$ of the distance in an hour. Compare the distances hiked by each person by matching the statements to the correct symbol. Each symbol may be used more than once or not at all.

$\frac{7}{10}$ ● $\frac{3}{6}$	$<$
$\frac{3}{8}$ ● $\frac{3}{6}$	$>$
$\frac{7}{10}$ ● $\frac{3}{8}$	$=$

6. Ramon is having some friends over after a baseball game. Ramon's job is to make a vegetable dip. The ingredients for the recipe are given.

Ingredients in Vegetable Dip

$\frac{3}{4}$ cup parsley	$\frac{5}{8}$ cup buttermilk
$\frac{1}{3}$ cup dill	$\frac{1}{2}$ cup cream cheese
$\frac{6}{8}$ cup scallions	$\frac{1}{12}$ cup lemon juice

Part A

Which ingredient does Ramon use the greater amount of, buttermilk or cream cheese? Explain how you found your answer.

Part B

Ramon says that he needs the same amount of two different ingredients. Is he correct? Support your answer with information from the problem.

STOP

Practice Test

Learning Objective
Show that addition and subtraction of fractions can be expressed as combining parts and separating parts referring to the same whole.

Name ______________________________

1. Cindy has two jars of paint. One jar is $\frac{3}{8}$ full. The other jar is $\frac{2}{8}$ full.

Use the fractions to write an equation that shows the amount of paint Cindy has.

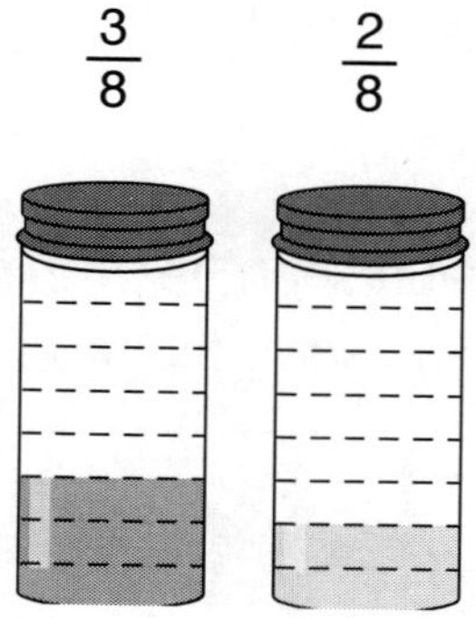

$\frac{1}{8}$	$\frac{2}{8}$	$\frac{3}{8}$	$\frac{5}{8}$	$\frac{7}{8}$

_____ + _____ = _____

2. On Monday, Erin measures $\frac{3}{4}$ inch of snowfall. It snows some more at the end of the day. Now there are $3\frac{1}{4}$ inches of snow. How many more inches of snow fell?

Part A

Draw a model for the problem. Then solve. Explain how your model helps you solve the problem.

Part B

On Tuesday, it snowed an additional $2\frac{2}{4}$ inches. How many total inches of snow fell on Monday and Tuesday? Show your work.

GO ON

Name ______________________________

3. On Saturday, Jesse plays basketball for $\frac{2}{3}$ hour. Then he plays some more. He plays $2\frac{1}{3}$ hours in all. How much longer did Jesse play basketball?

Part A

Draw a model to represent the problem. Then solve. Explain how your model helps you solve the problem.

Part B

On Sunday, Jesse played basketball for $1\frac{2}{3}$ hours. How many total hours did he play basketball on Saturday and Sunday? Show your work.

4. Betsy brought $\frac{6}{12}$ pound of trail mix on a camping trip. She ate $\frac{4}{12}$ pound of the trail mix. How much trail mix is left?

__________ pound

5. Mindi planted beans in $\frac{4}{10}$ of her garden and peas in $\frac{5}{10}$ of her garden. What fraction of the garden is filled with beans or peas?

Mindi's garden is __________ filled with beans or peas.

STOP

Name ______________________________

Practice Test
Learning Objective
Decompose fractions into a sum of fractions with like denominators.

1. Rita is making chili. The recipe calls for $2\frac{3}{4}$ cups of tomatoes. How many cups of tomatoes, written as a fraction greater than 1, are used in the recipe?

☐ cups

2. Lamar's mom sells sports equipment online. She sold $\frac{9}{10}$ of the sports equipment she had in stock. Select a way $\frac{9}{10}$ can be written as a sum of fractions. Mark all that apply.

Ⓐ $\frac{1}{10} + \frac{1}{10} + \frac{1}{10} + \frac{1}{10} + \frac{2}{10}$

Ⓑ $\frac{3}{10} + \frac{2}{10} + \frac{3}{10} + \frac{1}{10}$

Ⓒ $\frac{2}{10} + \frac{2}{10} + \frac{2}{10} + \frac{2}{10}$

Ⓓ $\frac{4}{10} + \frac{1}{10} + \frac{1}{10} + \frac{3}{10}$

Ⓔ $\frac{4}{10} + \frac{3}{10} + \frac{1}{10} + \frac{1}{10} + \frac{1}{10}$

Ⓕ $\frac{2}{10} + \frac{2}{10} + \frac{2}{10} + \frac{3}{10}$

3. Dillon's dad sells golf balls online. He sells $\frac{4}{5}$ of the golf balls he has in his attic. Select a way $\frac{4}{5}$ can be written as a sum of fractions. Mark all that apply.

Ⓐ $\frac{1}{5} + \frac{1}{5} + \frac{2}{5}$

Ⓑ $\frac{1}{5} + \frac{1}{5} + \frac{1}{5}$

Ⓒ $\frac{2}{5} + \frac{2}{5} + \frac{1}{5}$

Ⓓ $\frac{2}{5} + \frac{2}{5}$

Ⓔ $\frac{1}{5} + \frac{1}{5} + \frac{1}{5} + \frac{1}{5}$

Ⓕ $\frac{1}{5} + \frac{1}{5} + \frac{1}{5} + \frac{1}{5} + \frac{1}{5}$

4. Draw a line to show the mixed number and fraction that have the same value.

$1\frac{3}{4}$	$5\frac{1}{6}$	$3\frac{2}{5}$	$3\frac{1}{4}$
•	•	•	•
•	•	•	•
$\frac{13}{4}$	$\frac{16}{5}$	$\frac{31}{4}$	$\frac{17}{6}$

GO ON

Name ____________________

5. Draw a line to show the mixed number and fraction that have the same value.

$3\frac{2}{6}$	$4\frac{5}{8}$	$2\frac{3}{5}$	$2\frac{3}{8}$
$\frac{21}{8}$	$\frac{37}{3}$	$\frac{21}{4}$	$\frac{37}{8}$

6. Justin lives $4\frac{3}{5}$ miles from his grandfather's house. Write the mixed number as a fraction greater than 1.

$4\frac{3}{5} = \square$

7. Ilene is making smoothies. The recipe calls for $1\frac{1}{4}$ cups of strawberries. How many cups of strawberries, written as a fraction greater than 1, are used in the recipe?

_______ cups

8. Jane is leaving for vacation in $3\frac{4}{6}$ hours. Write the mixed number as a fraction greater than 1.

$3\frac{4}{6} = \square$

9. Mrs. Philbert is raising money for charity. She raises $\frac{7}{8}$ of the money she hoped to raise by asking her friends for donations. Select a way $\frac{7}{8}$ can be written as a sum of fractions. Mark all that apply.

Ⓐ $\frac{1}{8} + \frac{2}{8} + \frac{1}{8} + \frac{5}{8}$

Ⓑ $\frac{3}{8} + \frac{1}{8} + \frac{1}{8} + \frac{1}{8} + \frac{1}{8}$

Ⓒ $\frac{2}{8} + \frac{2}{8} + \frac{2}{8} + \frac{1}{8}$

Ⓓ $\frac{1}{8} + \frac{4}{8} + \frac{1}{8}$

Ⓔ $\frac{2}{8} + \frac{1}{8} + \frac{1}{8} + \frac{3}{8}$

Ⓕ $\frac{5}{8} + \frac{1}{8} + \frac{1}{8} + \frac{1}{8}$

STOP

Name ___________________________

Practice Test

Learning Objective
Add and subtract mixed numbers with like denominators using the properties of operations and the relationship between addition and subtraction.

1. Ivan biked $1\frac{2}{3}$ hours on Monday, $2\frac{1}{3}$ hours on Tuesday, and $2\frac{2}{3}$ hours on Wednesday. What is the total number of hours Ivan spent biking?

Ivan spent ☐ hours biking.

2. Tricia had $4\frac{1}{8}$ yards of fabric to make curtains. When she finished she had $2\frac{3}{8}$ yards of fabric left. She said she used $2\frac{2}{8}$ yards of fabric for the curtains. Do you agree? Explain.

3. Gina has $5\frac{2}{6}$ feet of silver ribbon and $2\frac{4}{6}$ of gold ribbon. How much more silver ribbon does Gina have than gold ribbon?

☐ feet more silver ribbon

4. Match the equation with the property used.

$\frac{3}{4} + \left(\frac{2}{4} + \frac{1}{4}\right) = \left(\frac{3}{4} + \frac{2}{4}\right) + \frac{1}{4}$ •

$\left(4\frac{1}{8} + \frac{1}{8}\right) + 2\frac{7}{8} = 4\frac{1}{8} + \left(\frac{1}{8} + 2\frac{7}{8}\right)$ •

$3\frac{1}{6} + 6 + 1\frac{3}{6} = 3\frac{1}{6} + 1\frac{3}{6} + 6$ •

$1\frac{4}{8} + 1\frac{1}{8} + 3\frac{6}{8} = 1\frac{1}{8} + 1\frac{4}{8} + 3\frac{6}{8}$ •

• Commutative Property

• Associative Property

GO ON

Name ______________________________

5. Jill is making a long cape. She needs $4\frac{1}{3}$ yards of blue fabric for the outside of the cape. She needs $3\frac{2}{3}$ yards of purple fabric for the lining of the cape.

Part A

Jill incorrectly subtracted the two mixed numbers to find how much more blue fabric than purple fabric she should buy. Her work is shown below.

$4\frac{1}{3} - 3\frac{2}{3} = \frac{12}{3} - \frac{9}{3} = \frac{3}{3}$

Why is Jill's work incorrect?

Part B

How much more blue fabric than purple fabric should Jill buy? Show your work.

6. Which statements are true? Mark all that apply.

Ⓐ $6\frac{1}{3} + 2\frac{2}{3}$ is equal to 10.

Ⓑ $1\frac{2}{8} + 3\frac{7}{8}$ is equal to $4\frac{1}{8}$.

Ⓒ $1\frac{3}{4} + 2\frac{2}{4}$ is equal to $4\frac{1}{4}$.

Ⓓ $9\frac{5}{6} - 3\frac{2}{6}$ is equal to $6\frac{3}{6}$.

STOP

Name ______________________________

Practice Test

Learning Objective
Solve word problems involving addition and subtraction of fractions with like denominators and referring to the same whole.

1. A painter mixed $\frac{1}{4}$ quart of red paint with $\frac{3}{4}$ quart of blue paint to make purple paint.

How much purple paint did the painter make?

[ ] quart of purple paint

2. Julia had $\frac{7}{10}$ gallon of lemonade. She gave some of the lemonade to her little sister. Now Julia has $\frac{3}{10}$ gallon of lemonade. How much lemonade did Julia give to her sister?

- (A) $\frac{10}{10}$ gallon
- (B) $\frac{5}{10}$ gallon
- (C) $\frac{4}{10}$ gallon
- (D) $\frac{3}{10}$ gallon

3. Each day, Tally's baby sister eats $\frac{1}{4}$ cup of rice cereal in the morning and $\frac{1}{4}$ cup of rice cereal in the afternoon.

It will take Tally's sister [2 / 3 / 4] days to eat 2 cups of rice cereal.

4. Henry ate $\frac{3}{8}$ of a sandwich. Keith ate $\frac{4}{8}$ of the same sandwich. How much more of the sandwich did Keith eat than Henry?

[ ] of the sandwich

GO ON

Name ______________________________

5. The school carnival is divided into sections. The dunk tanks are in $\frac{1}{10}$ of the carnival. Games are in $\frac{4}{10}$ of the carnival. Student exhibits are in $\frac{5}{10}$ of the carnival.

Part A

What fraction of the carnival is dunk tanks and games?

The fraction of the carnival with dunk tanks and games is ☐.

Part B

How much greater is the part of the carnival with student exhibits than the one with games? Explain how you could use a model to find the answer.

6. Jack has a jar of wax that is $\frac{1}{6}$ full. His dad gives him a second jar of wax that is $\frac{4}{6}$ full.

Use the fractions to write an equation to find the amount of wax Jack has.

$\frac{1}{6}$ $\frac{3}{6}$ $\frac{4}{6}$ $\frac{5}{6}$

☐ + ☐ = ☐

STOP

Name ______________________________

Practice Test

Learning Objective
Show that a fraction *a/b* is a multiple of 1/*b* and a whole number.

1. After $\frac{1}{8}$, what are the next four multiples of $\frac{1}{8}$?

2. Which fraction is a multiple of $\frac{1}{10}$? Mark all that apply.

Ⓐ $\frac{3}{10}$
Ⓑ $\frac{4}{10}$
Ⓒ $\frac{9}{12}$
Ⓓ $\frac{9}{8}$
Ⓔ $\frac{2}{10}$
Ⓕ $\frac{9}{10}$

3. Look at the number line. Write the missing fractions.

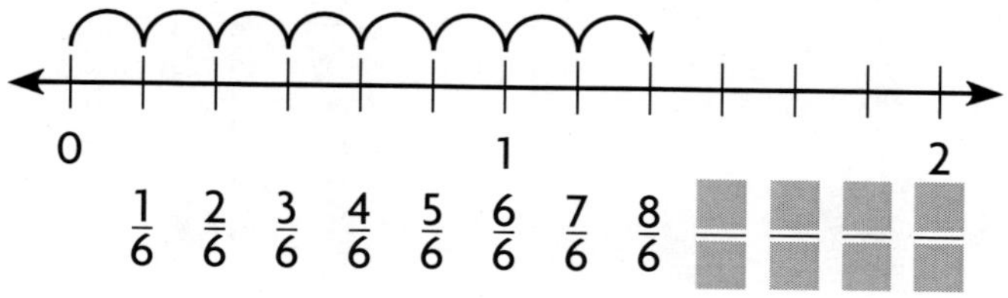

4. Which fraction is a multiple of $\frac{1}{8}$? Mark all that apply.

Ⓐ $\frac{3}{8}$
Ⓑ $\frac{8}{12}$
Ⓒ $\frac{2}{8}$
Ⓓ $\frac{4}{8}$
Ⓔ $\frac{8}{10}$
Ⓕ $\frac{8}{8}$

5. Look at the number line. Write the missing fractions.

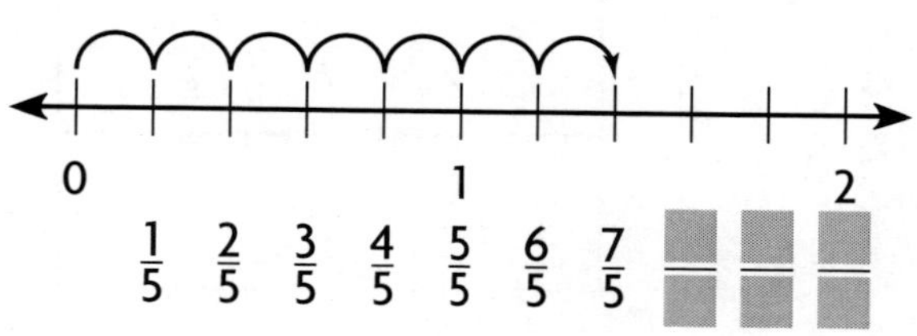

GO ON

Name ______________________________

6. After $\frac{1}{12}$, what are the next four multiples of $\frac{1}{12}$?

7. Which fraction is a multiple of $\frac{1}{5}$? Mark all that apply.

Ⓐ $\frac{4}{5}$

Ⓑ $\frac{5}{6}$

Ⓒ $\frac{5}{10}$

Ⓓ $\frac{3}{5}$

8. Represent the shaded part of the fraction bar as the product of a whole number and a unit fraction.

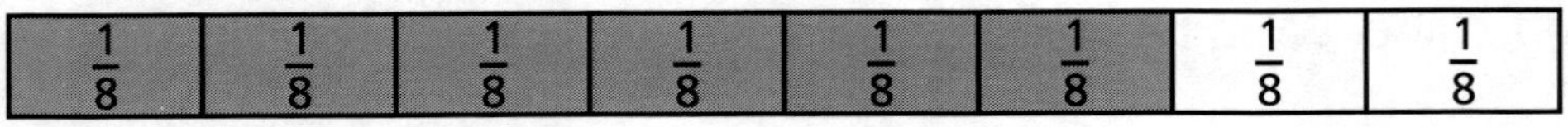

9. Complete the table to show the fraction as a product of a whole number and a unit fraction.

Fraction	Product
$\frac{5}{12}$	______
$\frac{2}{3}$	______
$\frac{4}{4}$	______

STOP

Name ________________________________

Practice Test

Learning Objective
Recognize that *a/b* is a multiple of 1/*b*, and use that fact to multiply a fraction by a whole number.

1. What fraction shows the product of $2 \times \frac{3}{5}$?

Ⓐ $\frac{10}{5}$

Ⓑ $\frac{6}{5}$

Ⓒ $\frac{5}{5}$

Ⓓ $\frac{6}{10}$

2. Asta wants to find the product of $3 \times \frac{4}{5}$.

Select a way to write $3 \times \frac{4}{5}$ as the product of a whole number and a unit fraction.

$3 \times \frac{4}{5} =$

$4 \times \frac{3}{5}$
$12 \times \frac{1}{5}$
$6 \times \frac{1}{5}$

3. Donna buys some fabric to make placemats. She uses 9 different types of fabric to make her design. She needs $\frac{1}{5}$ yard of each type of fabric. Use the following equation. Write the number in the box to make the statement true.

$$\frac{9}{5} = \underline{\hspace{3em}} \times \frac{1}{5}$$

4. Rico is making 4 batches of salsa. Each batch needs $\frac{2}{3}$ cup of corn. He only has a $\frac{1}{3}$-cup measure. How many times must Rico measure $\frac{1}{3}$ cup of corn to have enough for all of the salsa?

________ times

GO ON

Name ________________________________

5. Sarah is making 4 batches of granola bars. She adds $\frac{7}{8}$ cup peanuts to each batch. Her measuring cup holds $\frac{1}{8}$ cup. How many times must Sarah measure $\frac{1}{8}$ cup of peanuts to have enough for the granola bars?

Ⓐ 11 times

Ⓑ 16 times

Ⓒ 28 times

Ⓓ 32 times

6. Oleg wants to find the product of $4 \times \frac{2}{5}$.

Select a way to write $4 \times \frac{2}{5}$ as the product of a whole number and a unit fraction.

$4 \times \frac{2}{5} =$

$6 \times \frac{1}{5}$
$2 \times \frac{4}{5}$
$8 \times \frac{1}{5}$

7. Which fraction shows the product of $3 \times \frac{5}{6}$?

Ⓐ 5

Ⓑ $\frac{30}{6}$

Ⓒ $\frac{15}{6}$

Ⓓ $\frac{8}{6}$

STOP

Name ______________________________

Practice Test

Learning Objective
Solve word problems involving multiplication of a fraction by a whole number.

1. Molly is baking for the Moms and Muffins event at her school. She will bake 4 batches of banana muffins. She needs $\frac{3}{4}$ cups of bananas for each batch of muffins.

Part A

Molly completed the multiplication below and said she needed $1\frac{3}{4}$ cups of bananas for 4 batches of muffins. What is Molly's error?

$$4 \times \frac{3}{4} = 7 \times \frac{1}{4} = \frac{7}{4} = 1\frac{3}{4}$$

Part B

What is the correct number of cups Molly needs for 4 batches of muffins? Explain how you found your answer.

2. Theo is comparing shark lengths. He learned that a dogfish shark is $\frac{3}{5}$ meter long. A blue shark is 5 times as long as a dogfish shark. Find the length of a blue shark.

A blue shark is ☐ meters long.

3. Mimi recorded a play that lasted $\frac{2}{3}$ hour. She watched it 3 times over the weekend to study the lines. How many hours did Mimi spend watching the play? Show your work.

GO ON

Name ______________________________

4. Select the correct product for the equation.

$\frac{8}{16}$	$\frac{32}{8}$	$\frac{16}{8}$	$\frac{20}{8}$

$4 \times \frac{5}{8} = \square$ $\qquad$ $4 \times \frac{4}{8} = \square$

5. Mrs. Burnham is making modeling clay for her class. She needs $\frac{2}{3}$ cup of warm water for each batch.

Part A

Mrs. Burnham has a 1-cup measure that has no other markings. Can she make 6 batches of modeling clay using only the 1-cup measure? Describe two ways you can find the answer.

Part B

The modeling clay recipe also calls for $\frac{1}{2}$ cup of cornstarch. Nikki says Mrs. Burnham will also need 4 cups of cornstarch to make 6 batches of clay. Do you agree or disagree? Explain.

6. Mr. Tuyen uses $\frac{5}{8}$ of a tank of gas each week to drive to and from his job. How many tanks of gas does Mr. Tuyen use in 5 weeks? Write your answer two different ways.

Mr. Tuyen uses __________ or __________ tanks of gas.

STOP

Name ______________________________

Practice Test

Learning Objective
Show that a fraction with a denominator of 100 is a multiple of a fraction with a denominator of 10, and use this reasoning to add fractions with denominators of 10 and 100.

1. Henry is making a recipe for biscuits. The recipe calls for $\frac{5}{10}$ kilogram flour and $\frac{9}{100}$ kilogram sugar.

Part A

If Henry measures correctly and combines the two amounts, how much flour and sugar will he have? Show your work.

Part B

How can you write your answer as a decimal?

2. Ingrid is making a toy car. The toy car is $\frac{5}{10}$ meter high without the roof. The roof is $\frac{18}{100}$ meter high. What is the height of the toy car with the roof? Choose a number from each column to complete an equation to solve.

		Column 1		Column 2		Column 3	
		$\frac{5}{100}$		$\frac{18}{100}$		$\frac{68}{10}$	
$\frac{5}{10} + \frac{18}{100}$	$=$	$\frac{15}{100}$	$+$	$\frac{81}{100}$	$=$	$\frac{32}{100}$	meter high
		$\frac{50}{100}$		$\frac{18}{10}$		$\frac{68}{100}$	

3. Steve is measuring the growth of a tree. He drew this model to show the tree's growth in meters. Which fraction, mixed number, or decimal does the model show? Mark all that apply.

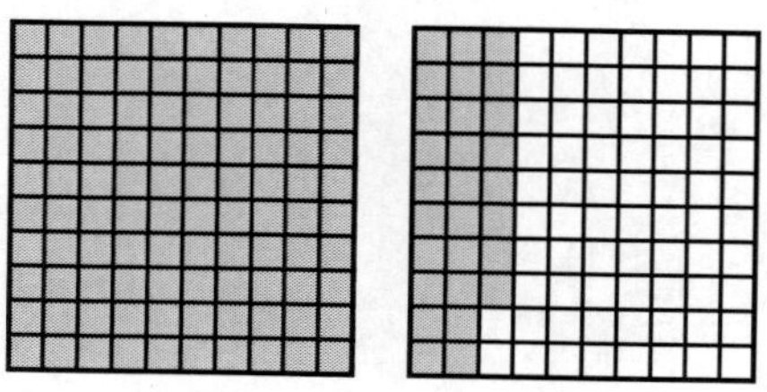

Ⓐ 1.28

Ⓑ 120.8

Ⓒ 0.28

Ⓓ $2\frac{8}{100}$

Ⓔ $1\frac{28}{100}$

Ⓕ $1\frac{28}{10}$

GO ON

Name ____________________

4 Jen is making a recipe for pancakes. The recipe calls for $\frac{4}{10}$ kilogram flour and $\frac{12}{100}$ kilogram sugar.

Part A

If Jen measures correctly and combines the two amounts, how much flour and sugar will she have? Show your work.

Part B

How can you write your answer as a decimal?

5. Jack drew a model to represent the number of miles from his home to the park. What decimal represents the part of the model that is shaded?

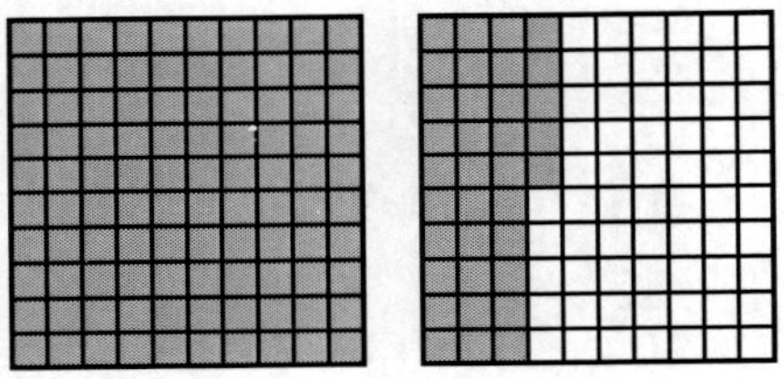

____

6. Charlie's model shows the number of hours he exercised yesterday. Which fraction, mixed number, or decimal does the model show? Mark all that apply.

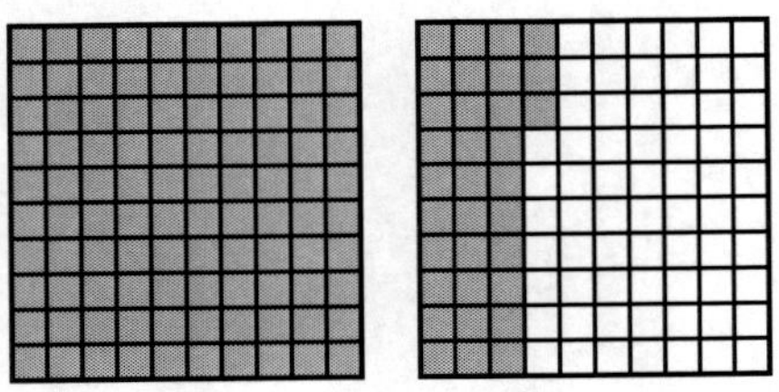

Ⓐ 1.33

Ⓑ $1\frac{33}{100}$

Ⓒ 133

Ⓓ $1\frac{3}{100}$

Ⓔ 13.03

Ⓕ $1\frac{33}{10}$

STOP

Name ______________________________

Practice Test

Learning Objective
Write tenths and hundredths as decimals and fractions, and use words, models, and standard form to represent numbers to hundredths.

1. Select a number shown by the model. Mark all that apply.

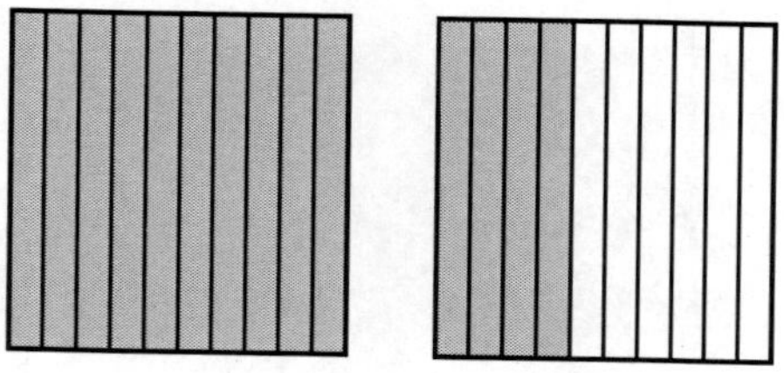

- $\frac{14}{10}$
- $\frac{40}{10}$
- 1.4
- $1\frac{4}{10}$
- 40
- 4.1

2. Shade the model to show $1\frac{52}{100}$. Then write the mixed number in decimal form.

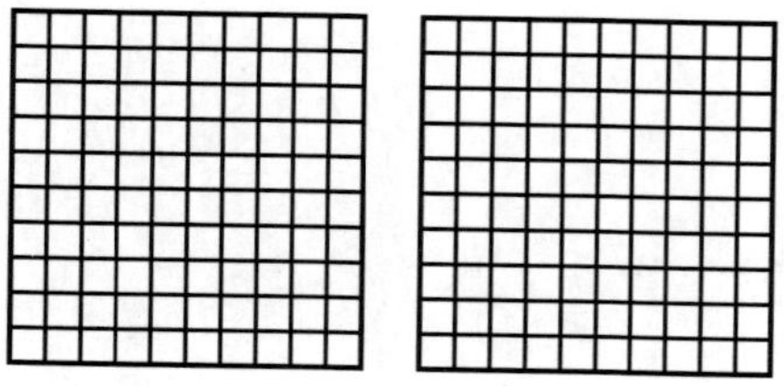

☐

3. Complete the table.

Bills and Coins	Money Amount ($)	Fraction or Mixed Number	Decimal
8 pennies		$\frac{8}{100}$	0.08
	$0.50		0.50
		$\frac{90}{100}$ or $\frac{9}{10}$	0.90
4 $1 bills 5 pennies			4.05

4. The point on the number line shows the number of seconds it took an athlete to run the 40-yard dash. Write the decimal that correctly names the point.

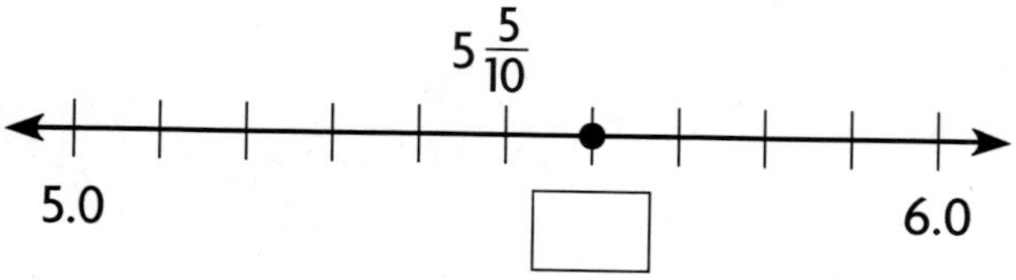

GO ON

Name ______________________________

5. Select a number shown by the model. Mark all that apply.

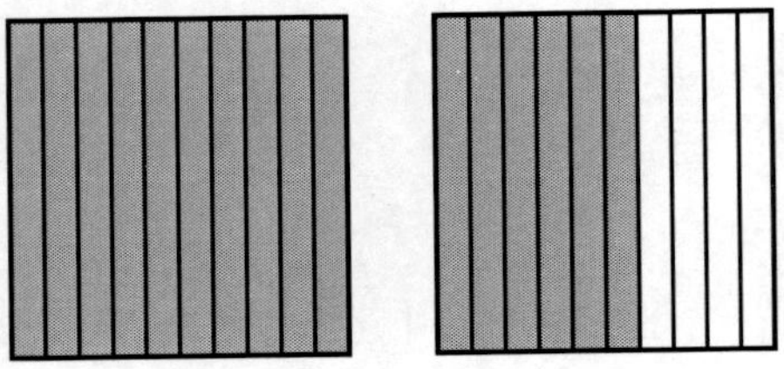

6.1	4.6	1.6
$\frac{60}{10}$	$\frac{16}{10}$	$1\frac{6}{10}$

6. Ryan sold a jigsaw puzzle at a yard sale for three dollars and five cents. Which names this money amount in terms of dollars? Mark all that apply.

Ⓐ 35.0

Ⓑ $3\frac{5}{100}$

Ⓒ \$3.05

Ⓓ 3.05

Ⓔ 3.50

Ⓕ $\frac{305}{10}$

7. Trisha walked $\frac{9}{10}$ of a mile to school. Shade the model. Then write the decimal to show how far Trisha walked.

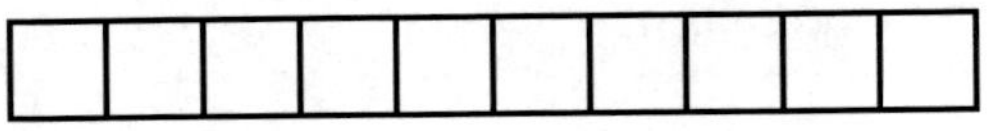

Trisha walked ________ mile to school.

8. Cora paid $\frac{65}{100}$ of a dollar to buy a postcard from Grand Canyon National Park in Arizona. What is $\frac{65}{100}$ written as a decimal in terms of dollars?

9. The U.S. Senate in Washington D.C. has 100 elected members. Last year, 30 senators ran for reelection. What decimal is equivalent to $\frac{30}{100}$?

STOP

Name ____

Practice Test

Learning Objective
Compare decimals to hundredths using $>$, $<$, or $=$.

1. Which inequalities are true? Mark all that apply.

Ⓐ $0.21 < 0.27$

Ⓑ $0.4 > 0.45$

Ⓒ $\$3.21 > \$0.20$

Ⓓ $1.9 < 1.90$

Ⓔ $6.2 > 6.02$

2. Luke lives 0.4 kilometer from a skating rink. Mark lives 0.25 kilometer from the skating rink.

Part A

Who lives closer to the skating rink? Explain.

Part B

How can you write each distance as a fraction? Explain.

Part C

Luke is walking to the skating rink to pick up a practice schedule. Then he will walk to Mark's house. Will he walk more than one kilometer or less than one kilometer? Explain.

GO ON

Name ______________________________

3. For numbers 3a–3b, choose the symbol that makes the statement true.

3a. 0.2 [$<$ / $>$ / $=$] 0.25

3b. 4.8 [$<$ / $>$ / $=$] 4.08

4. Gene lives 0.6 mile from school. Kate lives 0.51 mile from school.

Part A

Who lives closer to school? Explain.

Part B

How can you write each distance as a fraction? Explain.

Part C

Gene is walking to school to get a book he forgot. Then he will walk to Kate's house. Will he walk more than 1 mile or less than 1 mile? Explain.

Name ________________________________

Learning Objective
Identify relative sizes of measurement units, and express larger units in terms of smaller units, within one system of units.

1. Select the measures that are equal. Mark all that apply.

- Ⓐ 6 feet
- Ⓑ 15 yards
- Ⓒ 45 feet
- Ⓓ 600 inches
- Ⓔ 12 feet
- Ⓕ 540 inches

2. Jackie made 6 quarts of lemonade. Jackie says she made 3 pints of lemonade. Explain Jackie's error. Then find the correct number of pints of lemonade.

3. Sabita made this table to relate two customary units of liquid volume.

______	______
1	2
2	4
3	6
4	8
5	10

Part A

List the number pairs for the table. Then describe the relationship between the numbers in each pair.

Part B

Label the columns of the table. Explain your answer.

GO ON

Name ______________________________

4. Draw lines to match equivalent time intervals. Items may be matched more than once or not at all.

$\frac{1}{2}$ hour	2 hours	3 hours	8 hours	72 hours
•	•	•	•	•
•	•	•	•	•
3 days	180 minutes	1,800 seconds	480 minutes	60 minutes

5. Mrs. DeMarco wants to estimate the height of her garage door. Select the best benchmark for her to use.

(A) the width of a paperclip

(B) the length of a baseball bat

(C) the height of a license plate

(D) the distance she can walk in 20 minutes

6. Lauren bought two items to make dinner. She says the difference in mass between the items she bought is 4,000 grams. Which two items did Lauren buy?

(A) turkey: 6 kilograms

(B) crate of apples: 8 kilograms

(C) bag of ears of corn: 3 kilograms

(D) bag of sweet potatoes: 2 kilograms

(E) bag of stuffing: 1 kilogram

7. Write the equivalent measurements in each column.

2,000 millimeters	200 centimeters	20 centimeters
$\frac{25}{100}$ meter	0.200 meter	0.25 meter
$\frac{200}{1,000}$ meter	250 millimeters	20 decimeters

2 meters	25 centimeters	200 decimeters

STOP

Name ______________________________

Practice Test
Learning Objective
Solve word problems using the four operations involving money, mass, and time.

1. After selling some old books and toys, Gwen and her brother Max had 5 one-dollar bills, 6 quarters, and 8 dimes. They agreed to divide the money equally.

Part A

What is the total amount of money that Gwen and Max earned? Explain.

Part B

Max said that he and Gwen cannot get equal amounts of money because 5 one-dollar bills cannot be divided evenly. Do you agree with Max? Explain.

2. Kylee and two of her friends are at a museum. They find $3.63 on the ground. If Kylee and her friends share the money equally, how much will each person get?

Each person will get ________

GO ON

Name ______________________________

3. Tran has $5.82. He is saving for a video game that costs $9.

Tran needs ________ more to have enough money for the game.

4. Wendy is making potato salad for a picnic. One sack of potatoes weighs 14 pounds. What is the weight of a sack of potatoes in ounces?

________ ounces

5. Anya arrived at the library on Saturday morning at 11:10 A.M. She left the library 1 hour 20 minutes later. Draw jumps on the time line to show the end time.

Anya left the library at ________ P.M.

6. Chaz needs $4.77 for new batteries. He has $3. He needs ________ more to have enough money for the batteries.

7. Kyle is practicing for a 1-mile race. His normal time is 8 minutes 8 seconds. What is Kyle's normal time, in seconds?

________ seconds

STOP

Name ________________________________

Practice Test

Learning Objective
Solve word problems involving area of rectangles using area and perimeter formulas.

1. Maura wants to make a rectangular picture frame with a perimeter of 50 inches. Which pairs of dimensions could she use? Mark all that apply.

   Ⓐ length: 25 inches   width: 2 inches
   Ⓑ length: 20 inches   width: 5 inches
   Ⓒ length: 17 inches   width: 8 inches
   Ⓓ length: 15 inches   width: 5 inches
   Ⓔ length: 15 inches   width: 10 inches

2. The swimming club's indoor pool is in a rectangular building. Marco is laying tile around the rectangular pool.

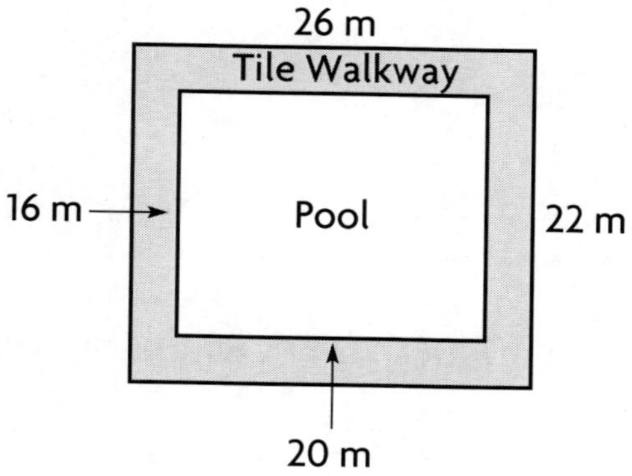

Part A

What is the area of the pool and the combined area of the pool and the walkway? Show your work.

Part B

How many square meters of tile will Marco need for the walkway? Explain how you found your answer.

GO ON

Name ______________________________

3. Ms. Bennett wants to buy carpeting for her living room and dining room.

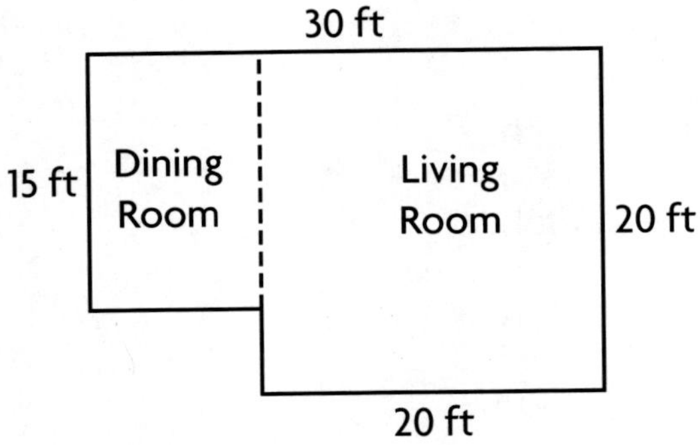

Explain how she can find the amount of carpet she needs to cover the floor in both rooms. Then find the amount of carpet she will need.

4. Which rectangle has a perimeter of 10 feet? Mark all that apply.

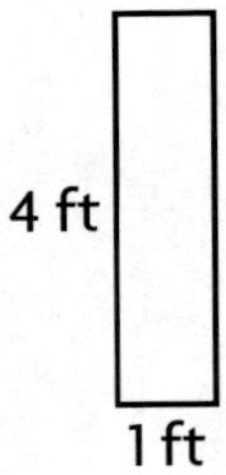

Ⓐ

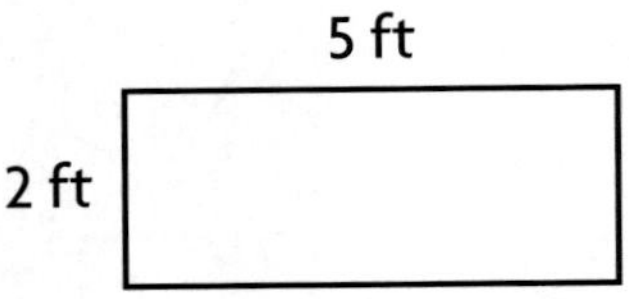

Ⓑ

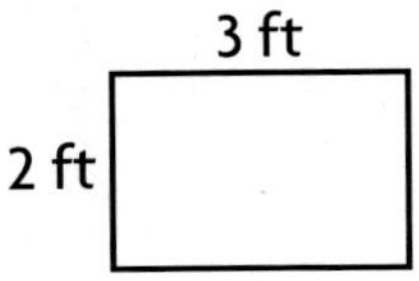

Ⓒ

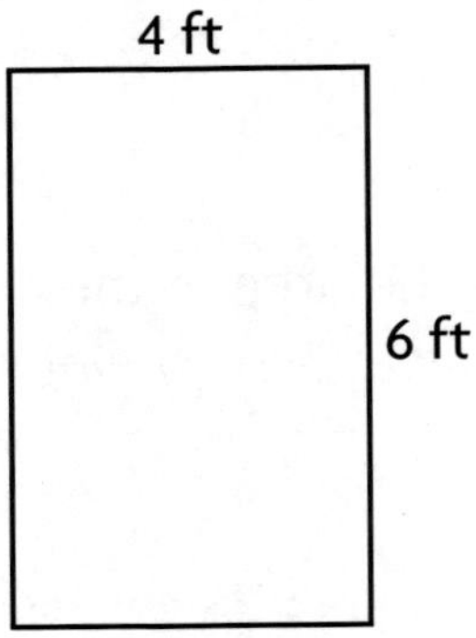

Ⓓ

5. Tricia is cutting her initial from a piece of felt. Which expressions correctly complete the statement?

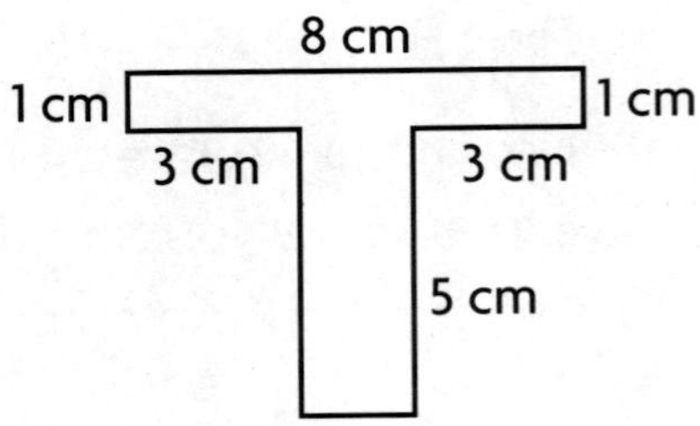

Tricia can add the products of [1×8 / 3×5 / 1×5] and [5×2 / 1×3 / 2×3] to find the square centimeters of felt she needs.

STOP

Name ______________________________

Practice Test

Learning Objective
Make a line plot to display measurement data, and solve addition and subtraction problems using the data.

1. Josh practices gymnastics each day after school. The data shows the lengths of time Josh practiced gymnastics for 2 weeks.

Time Practicing Gymnastics (in hours)
$\frac{1}{4}, \frac{1}{4}, \frac{3}{4}, \frac{3}{4}, \frac{1}{2}, 1, 1, 1, \frac{3}{4}, 1$

Part A

Make a tally table and line plot to show the data.

Time Practicing Gymnastics	
Time (in hours)	Tally

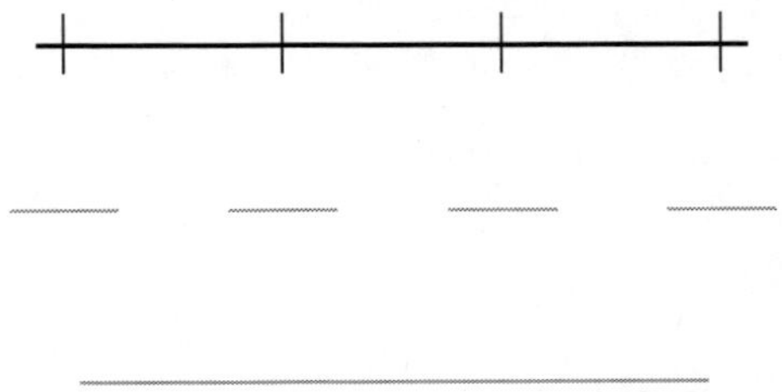

Part B

Explain how you used the tally table to label the numbers and plot the Xs.

Part C

What is the difference between the longest time and shortest time Josh spent practicing gymnastics?

_______ hour

GO ON

Name ______________________________

2. Leah has cheerleading practice each day after school. The data shows the lengths of time Leah had practice for 2 weeks.

Time at Cheerleading Practice (in hours)
$\frac{1}{3}$, $\frac{1}{3}$, $\frac{2}{3}$, $\frac{2}{3}$, $\frac{2}{3}$,
1, 1, 1, $\frac{1}{3}$, 1

Part A

Make a tally table and line plot to show the data.

Time at Cheerleading Practice	
Time (in hours)	Tally

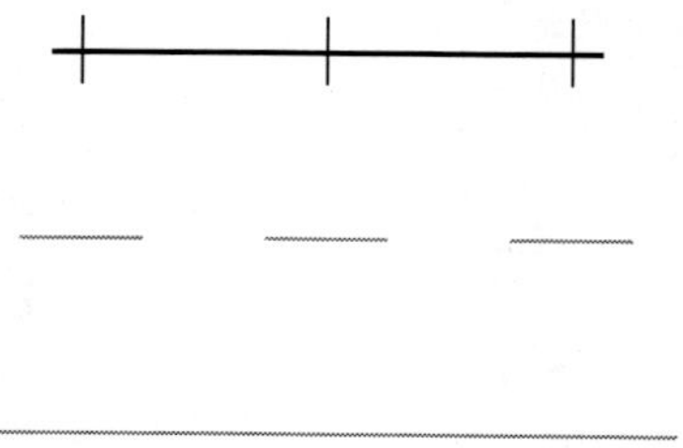

Part B

What is the difference between the longest time and shortest time Leah spent at cheerleading practice?

________ hour

3. The table shows the distances some students walked to school. Complete the line plot to show the data.

Distance Students Walked (in miles)
$\frac{1}{5}$, $\frac{2}{5}$, $\frac{3}{5}$, $\frac{3}{5}$, $\frac{5}{5}$, $\frac{3}{5}$,
$\frac{2}{5}$, $\frac{4}{5}$, $\frac{3}{5}$, $\frac{1}{5}$, $\frac{4}{5}$, $\frac{4}{5}$

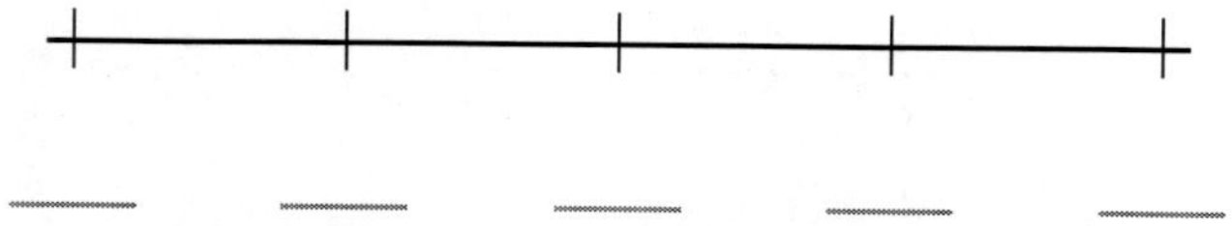

Distance Students Walked (in miles)

How many students walked less than 1 mile to school?

________ students

STOP

Name ______________________________

Practice Test

Learning Objective
Show that an angle that turns through *n* one-degree angles has an angle measure of *n* degrees.

1. An angle represents $\frac{1}{12}$ of a circle. Use the numbers to show how to find the measure of the angle in degrees.

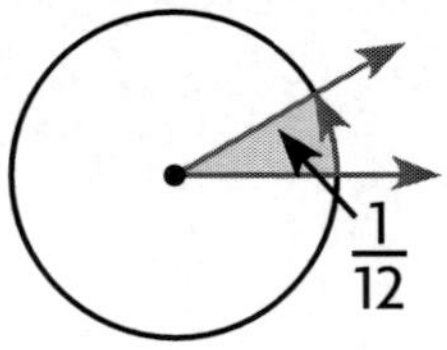

$$\frac{1}{12} = \frac{1 \times \square}{12 \times \square} = \frac{\square}{360}$$

The angle measure is ______.

2. For numbers 2a–2b, select the fraction that makes a true statement about the figure.

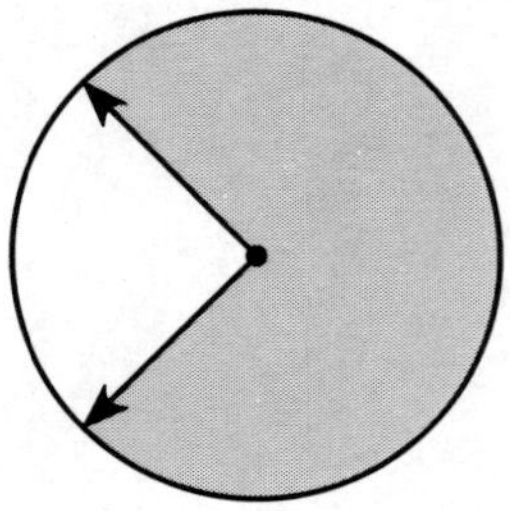

Figure 1

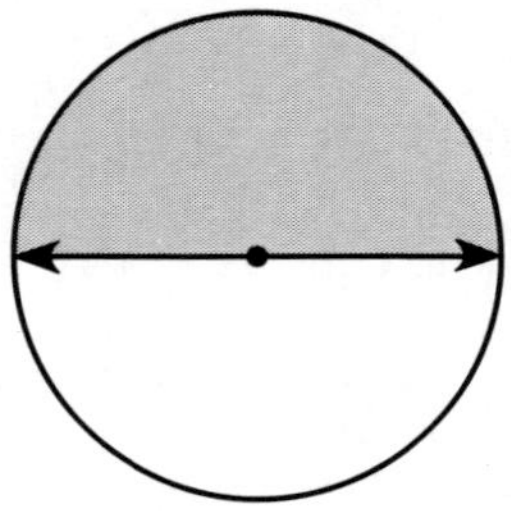

Figure 2

2a. The angle in Figure 1 represents a [$\frac{1}{4}$ / $\frac{1}{2}$ / $\frac{3}{4}$] turn.

2b. The angle in Figure 2 represents a [$\frac{1}{4}$ / $\frac{1}{2}$ / $\frac{3}{4}$] turn.

3. An angle represents $\frac{1}{10}$ of a circle. Use the numbers to show how to find the measure of the angle in degrees.

$$\frac{1}{10} = \frac{1 \times \square}{10 \times \square} = \frac{\square}{360}$$

The angle measure is ______.

GO ON

Name ___________________________________

4. An angle measures 125°. Through what fraction of a circle does the angle turn?

$\frac{\square}{\square}$ of a circle

5. Write the letter for each angle measure in the correct box.

Ⓐ 125° Ⓑ 90° Ⓒ 180° Ⓓ 30° Ⓔ 45° Ⓕ 95°

acute	obtuse	right	straight

6. Write the letter for each angle measure in the correct box.

Ⓐ 20° Ⓑ 77° Ⓒ 111° Ⓓ 180° Ⓔ 175° Ⓕ 90°

acute	obtuse	right	straight

7. A gear in a watch turns clockwise, in one-degree sections, a total of 300 times.

The gear has turned a total of ☐ degrees.

8. A carousel turns counterclockwise, in one-degree sections, a total of 280 times.

The carousel has turned a total of ☐ degrees.

STOP

Name ______________________________

Practice Test
Learning Objective
Measure angles in whole-number degrees using appropriate tools.

1. Use a protractor to find the measure of the angle.

The angle measures ______.

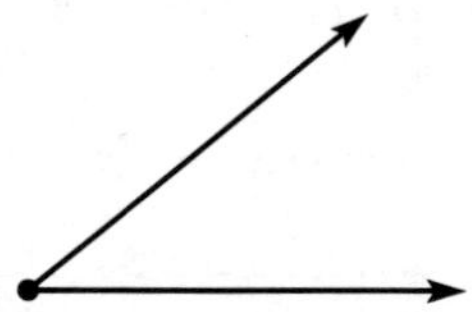

2. Use a protractor to find the measure of each angle. Write each angle and its measure in a box ordered by the measure of the angles from least to greatest.

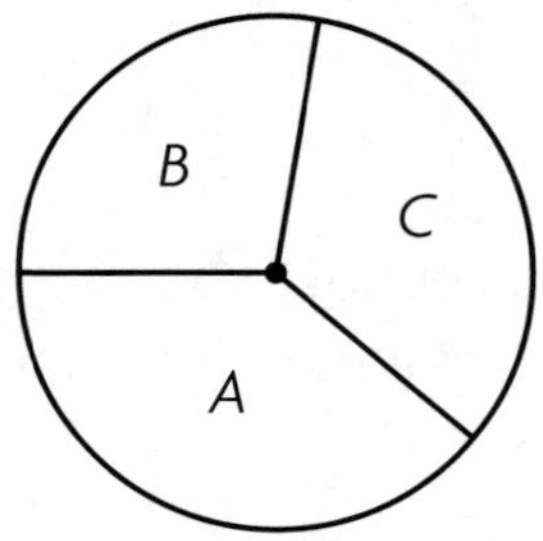

Angle:	Angle:	Angle:
Measure:	Measure:	Measure:

3. Choose the word or number to complete a true statement about $\angle JKL$.

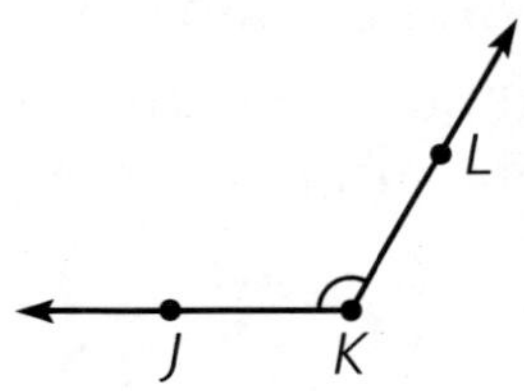

$\angle JKL$ is a(n) [acute / obtuse / right] angle that has a measure of [60°. / 120°. / 135°.]

GO ON

Name ______________________________

4. Use a protractor to find the measures of the unknown angles.

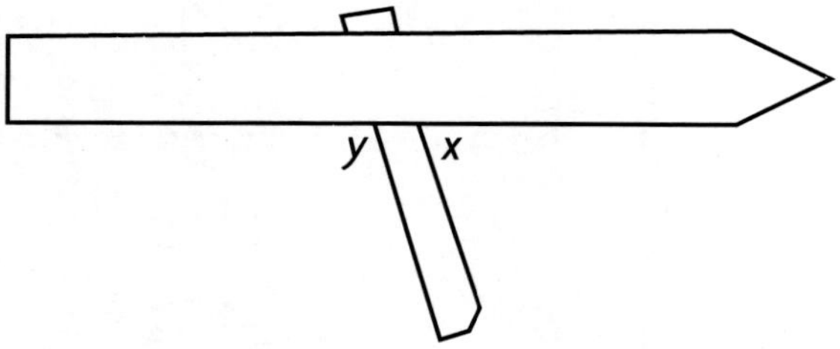

$m\angle x =$ _____ $m\angle y =$ _____

What do you notice about the measures of the unknown angles? Is this what you would have expected? Explain your reasoning.

5. Use a protractor to find the measure of each angle. Write each angle and its measure in a box ordered by the measure of the angles from least to greatest.

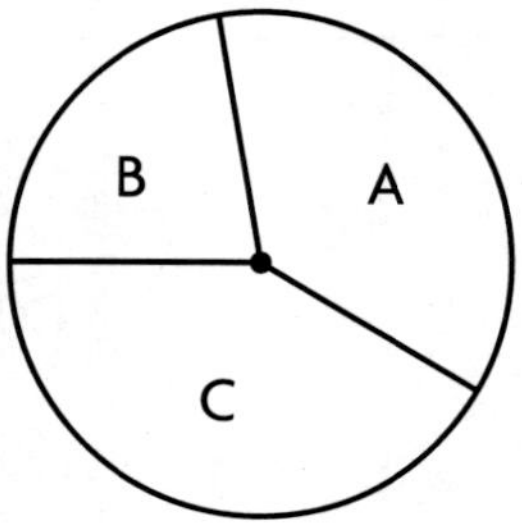

Angle: Measure:	Angle: Measure:	Angle: Measure:

STOP

Name ____________________

Learning Objective
Solve addition and subtraction word and mathematical problems showing that when an angle is decomposed into parts, the sum of the parts is equal to the original angle measure.

1. Match the measure of each $\angle C$ with the measure of $\angle D$ that forms a straight angle.

$\angle C$	$\angle D$
	145°
122°	75°
35°	148°
62°	58°
105°	55°
	118°

2. Renee drew the figure shown. Which statements are true? Mark all that apply.

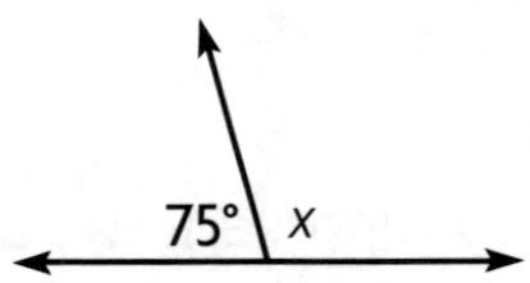

Ⓐ The measure of a straight angle is 180°.

Ⓑ To find the measure of angle *x*, Renee can subtract 75° from 180°.

Ⓒ The measure of angle *x* is 115°.

Ⓓ The measure of angle *x* is 105°.

3. A circle is divided into parts. Which sum could represent the angle measures that make up the circle? Mark all that apply.

Ⓐ 120° + 120° + 120°

Ⓑ 47° + 61° + 78° + 83° + 101°

Ⓒ 15° + 40° + 53° + 62° + 90° + 100°

Ⓓ 20° + 30° + 60° + 70°

GO ON

Name ____________________

4. Use the numbers and symbols to write an equation that can be used to find the measure of the unknown angle.

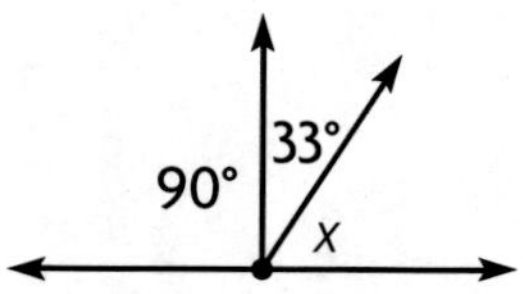

33	45	90	180
x	=	+	×

What is the measure of the unknown angle? ______

5. Melanie cuts a rectangle out of a piece of scrap paper as shown. She wants to calculate the angle measure of the piece that is left over.

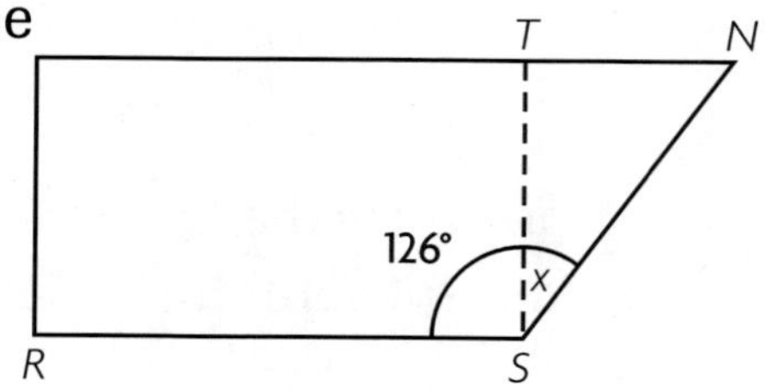

Part A

Draw a bar model to represent the problem.

Part B

Write and solve an equation to find x.

The angle measures ______.

6. A circle is divided into parts. Which sum could represent the angle measures that make up the circle? Mark all that apply.

Ⓐ 120° + 120° + 120° + 120°

Ⓑ 33° + 82° + 111° + 50° + 84°

Ⓒ 25° + 40° + 80° + 105° + 110°

Ⓓ 40° + 53° + 72° + 81° + 90° + 34°

Name ______________________

Practice Test

Learning Objective
Identify and draw points, line segments, lines, angles, rays, and parallel and perpendicular lines using appropriate tools.

1. Gavin is designing a kite. He sketched a picture of the kite. How many right angles does the kite appear to have?

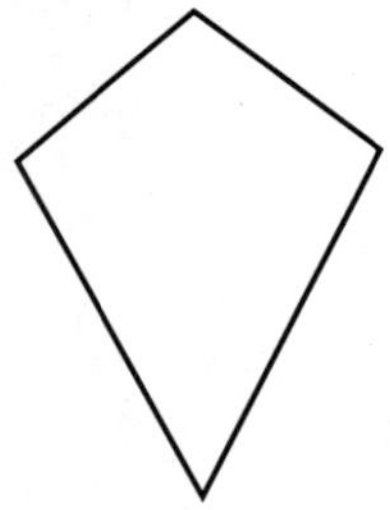

_____ right angles

2. Write the word that describes each part of Figure A written below.

ray | line | line segment | acute angle | right angle

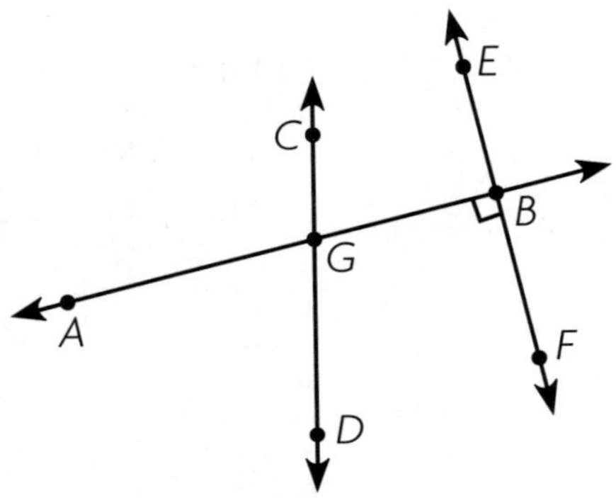

Figure A

$\overline{EB}$ ______________

$\overleftrightarrow{AB}$ ______________

$\overrightarrow{GA}$ ______________

$\angle EBG$ ______________

$\angle CGB$ ______________

3. Choose the labels to make a true statement.

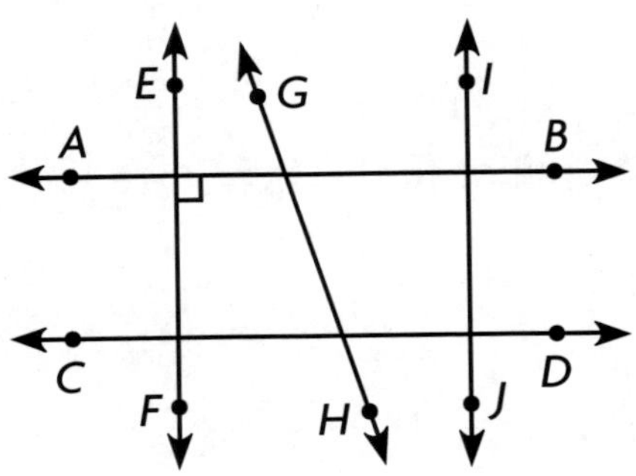

[$\overleftrightarrow{GH}$ / $\overleftrightarrow{CD}$ / $\overleftrightarrow{AB}$] is parallel to [$\overleftrightarrow{EF}$ / $\overleftrightarrow{CD}$ / $\overleftrightarrow{GH}$].

GO ON

Name ______________________________

4. Mike drew a figure with opposite sides parallel. Write the pairs of parallel sides. What figure is it?

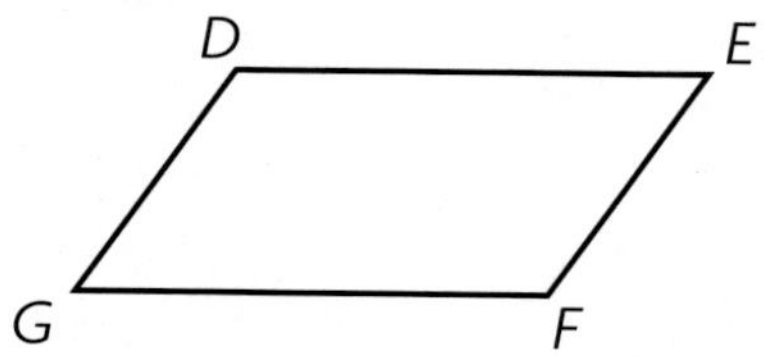

5. What term best describes the figure shown below?

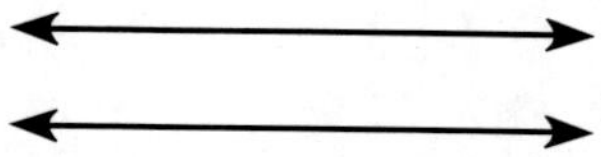

6. Choose the labels to make a true statement.

$\overleftrightarrow{GH}$ $\overleftrightarrow{IJ}$ $\overleftrightarrow{AB}$	is parallel to	$\overleftrightarrow{AB}$ $\overleftrightarrow{CD}$ $\overleftrightarrow{GH}$	.

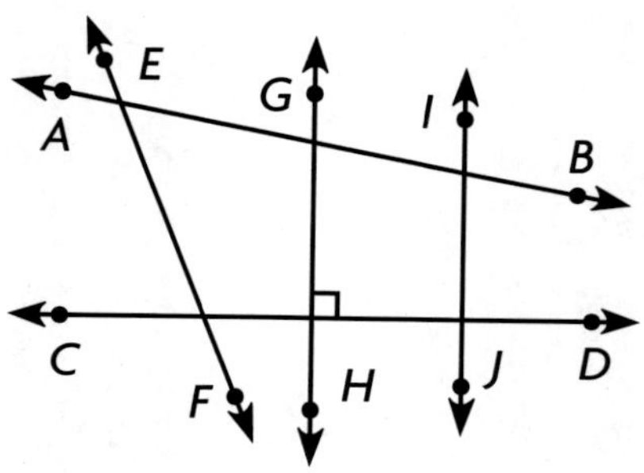

7. Lisa drew a figure with two sides perpendicular. Write the pair of perpendicular sides. What figure is it?

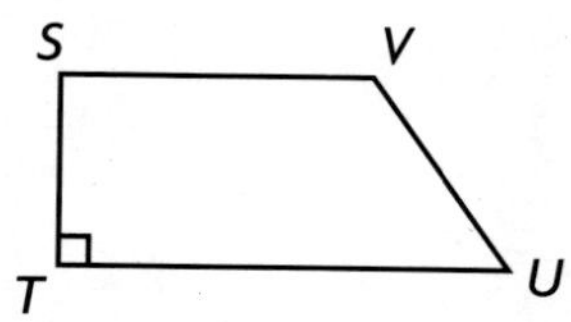

STOP

Name ______________________________

Practice Test

Learning Objective
Classify triangles and quadrilaterals based on the presence of parallel or perpendicular lines or the presence of certain types of angles.

1. Classify the figure. Select all that apply.

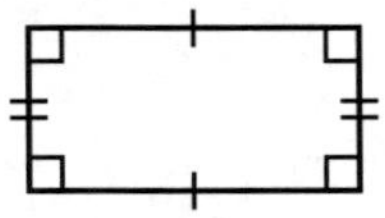

Ⓐ quadrilateral
Ⓑ trapezoid
Ⓒ parallelogram
Ⓓ rectangle
Ⓔ rhombus
Ⓕ square

2. Jeremy drew Figure 1, and Louisa drew Figure 2.

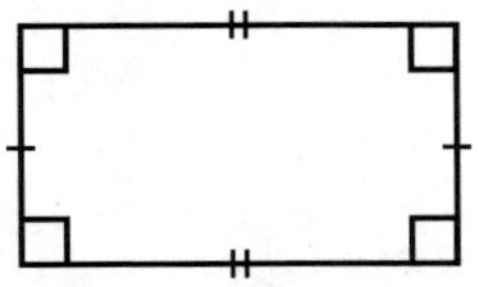

Figure 1

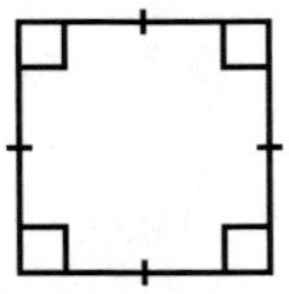

Figure 2

Part A

Jeremy says both figures are rectangles. Do you agree with Jeremy? Support your answer.

Part B

Louisa says both figures are rhombuses. Do you agree with Louisa? Support your answer.

GO ON

Name ______________________________

3. Write the letter of the triangle under its correct classification.

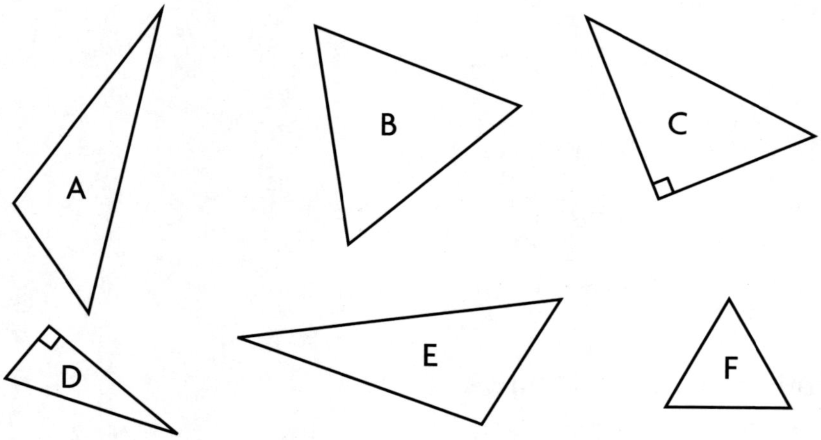

Acute Triangle	Obtuse Triangle	Right Triangle

4. Jessica made a pennant that looks like a triangle. How can you classify the triangle based upon its angles?

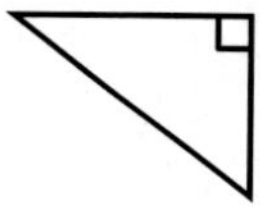

The triangle is a(n) ________ triangle.

5. Alison has a sticker that looks like a quadrilateral that has 2 pairs of parallel sides and no right angles. How can you classify the figure?

The quadrilateral is a ________________.

STOP

Name ______________________________

Learning Objective
Recognize and draw lines of symmetry in two-dimensional figures.

1. Naomi leaves for her trip to Los Angeles on the 12th day of August. Since August is the 8th month, Naomi wrote the date as shown.

8 / 12

Naomi says all the numbers she wrote have line symmetry. Is she correct? Explain your thinking.

2. Match each figure with the correct number of lines of symmetry it has.

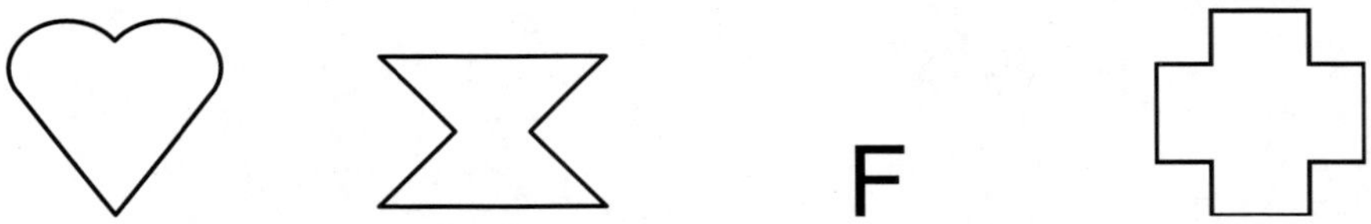

A	B	C	D
0 lines of symmetry	1 line of symmetry	2 lines of symmetry	More than 2 lines of symmetry

3. Claudia drew the figure below. Draw a line of symmetry on Claudia's figure.

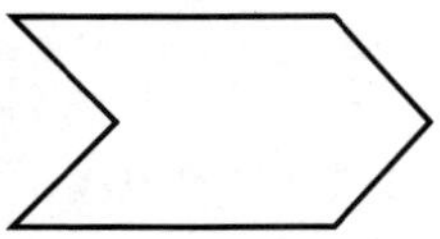

GO ON

Name ______________________________

4. Debbie leaves for her trip to San Diego on the 13th day of July. Since July is the 7th month, Debbie wrote the date as shown.

7 / 13

Debbie says all the numbers she wrote have line symmetry. Is she correct? Explain your thinking.

5. Match each figure with the correct number of lines of symmetry it has.

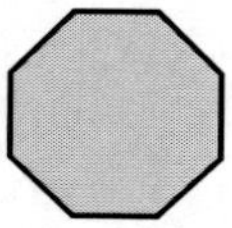		**S**	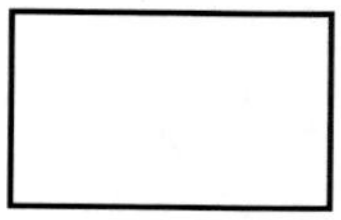
A	B	C	D

0 lines of symmetry	1 line of symmetry	2 lines of symmetry	More than 2 lines of symmetry
☐	☐	☐	☐

6. Circle the letter that does not have line symmetry.

FEET

7. Jared found the number of lines of symmetry for the figure. How many lines of symmetry does it have?

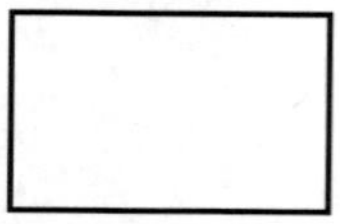

_______ lines of symmetry

STOP

1. Jay and Blair went fishing. Together, they caught 27 fish. Jay caught 2 times as many fish as Blair. How many fish did Jay and Blair each catch? Write an equation and solve. Explain your work.

2. Write the letter of the triangle under its correct classification.

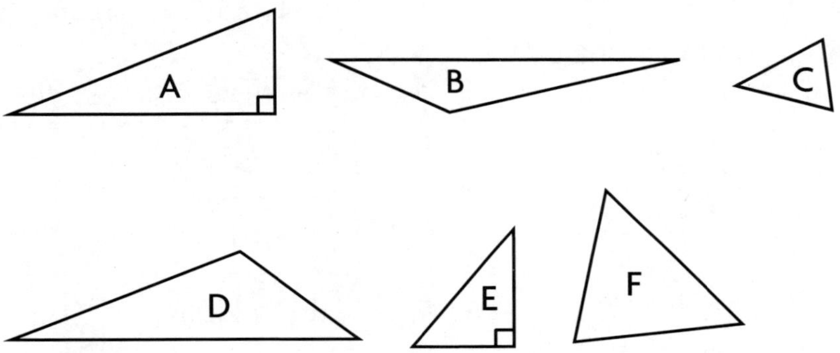

Acute Triangle	Obtuse Triangle	Right Triangle

3. Rick has one dollar and twenty-seven cents to buy a notebook. Which names this money amount? Mark all that apply.

- Ⓐ 12.7
- Ⓑ 1.027
- Ⓒ \$1.27
- Ⓓ 1.27
- Ⓔ $1\frac{27}{100}$
- Ⓕ $\frac{127}{10}$

4. Use the rule to write the first five terms of the pattern.

Rule: Add 7, subtract 4 First term: 5

____

GO ON

Name ___________________________

5. Liam has 3 boxes of baseball cards with 50 cards in each box. He also has 5 boxes with 40 basketball cards in each box. If Liam goes to the store and buys 50 more baseball cards, how many baseball and basketball cards does Liam have? Show your work.

6. The table shows the distances of some places in town from the school.

From least to greatest, order the locations by their distance from school.

Distance from School	
Place	**Distance**
Library	$\frac{3}{5}$ mile
Post Office	$\frac{1}{2}$ mile
Park	$\frac{3}{4}$ mile
Town Hall	$\frac{8}{10}$ mile

7. Classify the numbers. Some numbers may belong in more than one box.

54 72 84 90 96

Divisible by 5 and 9	Divisible by 6 and 9	Divisible by 2 and 6

8. Alma is making 3 batches of tortillas. Each batch needs $\frac{3}{4}$ cup of water. She only has a $\frac{1}{4}$-cup measure. How many times must Alma measure $\frac{1}{4}$ cup of water to have enough for all of the tortillas?

_______ times

GO ON

9. Mrs. Miller wants to estimate the width of the steps in front of her house. Select the best benchmark for her to use.

Ⓐ her fingertip

Ⓑ the thickness of a dime

Ⓒ the width of a license plate

Ⓓ how far she can walk in 20 minutes

10. Mr. Rodriguez bought 420 pencils for the school. If there are 10 pencils in a box, how many boxes did he buy?

Ⓐ 42 Ⓒ 430

Ⓑ 420 Ⓓ 4,200

11. Miguel's class went to the state fair. The fairground is divided into sections. Rides are in $\frac{6}{10}$ of the fairground. Games are in $\frac{2}{10}$ of the fairground. Farm exhibits are in $\frac{1}{10}$ of the fairground.

Part A

What fraction of the fairground is rides and games? ☐

Part B

How much greater is the part of the fairground with rides than farm exhibits? Explain how a model could be used to find the answer.

GO ON

Name ______________________________

12. Match the measure of each $\angle R$ with the measure of $\angle S$ that forms a right angle.

$\angle R$	$\angle S$
25° •	• 65°
	• 75°
44° •	• 39°
	• 58°
51° •	• 46°
38° •	• 52°

13. Select a number for ■ that will make a true comparison. Mark all that apply.

seven hundred three thousand, two hundred nine > ■

Ⓐ 702,309 Ⓒ 703,209 Ⓔ 730,029

Ⓑ 703,029 Ⓓ 703,290 Ⓕ 730,209

14. Kyleigh put a large rectangular sticker on her notebook. The height of the sticker measures 18 centimeters. The base is half as long as the height. What area of the notebook does the sticker cover?

__________ square centimeters

15. Veronica found the number of lines of symmetry for the figure below. How many lines of symmetry does it have?

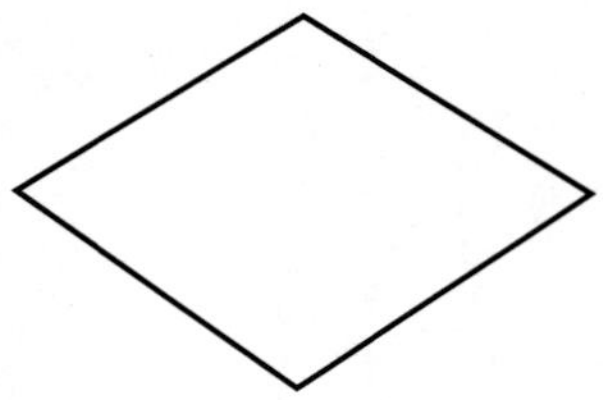

_______ lines of symmetry

GO ON

Name ______________________________

16. Lexi, Susie, and Rial are playing an online word game. Rial scores 100,034 points. Lexi scores 9,348 fewer points than Rial and Susie scores 9,749 more points than Lexi. What is Susie's score? Show your work.

17. Tenley makes stained glass windows. She used this piece of stained glass in one of the windows. How many right angles does this piece of stained glass appear to have?

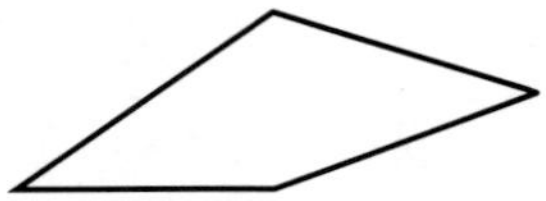

______ right angles

18. Tara has softball practice Tuesday, Wednesday, Thursday, and Sunday. Each practice is $1\frac{1}{3}$ hours. Tara says she will have practice for 3 hours this week.

Part A

Without multiplying, explain how you know Tara is incorrect.

Part B

How long will Tara have softball practice this week? Write your answer as a mixed number. Show your work.

GO ON

19. There are 2,571 fish in a lake. That is 3 times the number of fish that lived in the lake 5 years ago. How many fish lived in the lake 5 years ago? Write an equation. Then solve.

20. For numbers 20a–20b, use place value to find the product.

20a. $3 \times 600 = 3 \times$ ☐ hundreds

$=$ ☐ hundreds

$=$ ☐

20b. $5 \times 400 = 5 \times$ ☐ hundreds

$=$ ☐ hundreds

$=$ ☐

21. The table shows the distances some students hiked. Complete the line plot to show the data.

Distance Students Hiked (in miles)
$\frac{4}{8}$, $\frac{5}{8}$, $\frac{7}{8}$, $\frac{7}{8}$, $\frac{5}{8}$, $\frac{6}{8}$, $\frac{7}{8}$, $\frac{7}{8}$, $\frac{6}{8}$

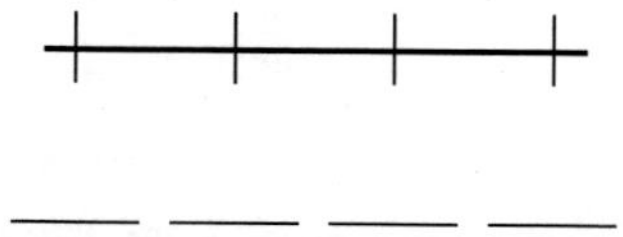

Distance Students Hiked

GO ON

Name ______________________________

22. Hamid's soccer game will start at 11:00 A.M., but the players must arrive at the field three-quarters of an hour early to warm up. Hamid says he has to be at the field at 9:45 A.M. Is Hamid correct? Explain your answer.

23. On field day, Danny captured 6 times as many flags as Jon during a game of Capture the Flag. Together, they captured 14 flags. How many flags did each person capture? Complete the bar model. Write an equation and solve.

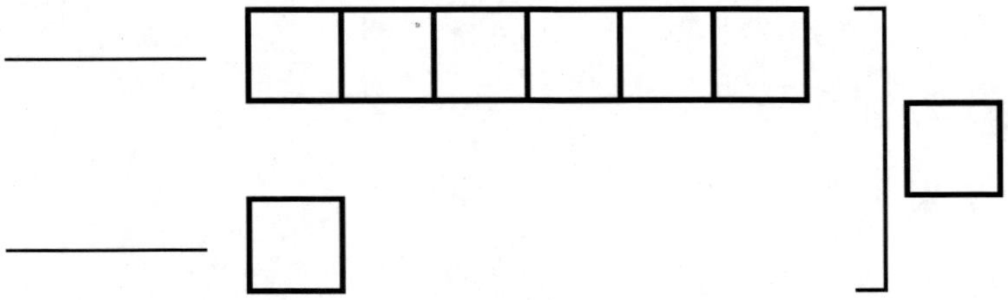

24. For numbers 24a–24d, write a fraction from the tiles to make a true equation.

$\frac{1}{10}$ $\frac{2}{10}$ $\frac{3}{10}$ $\frac{4}{10}$

24a. $\frac{10}{10} = \frac{5}{10} + \frac{3}{10} + \square$

24b. $1 = \frac{1}{10} + \frac{5}{10} + \square$

24c. $\frac{7}{10} = \frac{1}{10} + \frac{1}{10} + \frac{1}{10} + \frac{1}{10} + \square$

24d. $\frac{4}{10} = \frac{1}{10} + \frac{1}{10} + \frac{1}{10} + \square$

GO ON

Name ______________________________

25. Taylor cuts $\frac{1}{2}$ sheet of construction paper for an arts and crafts project. Write $\frac{1}{2}$ as an equivalent fraction with the denominators shown.

$\frac{\square}{4}$ $\frac{\square}{6}$ $\frac{\square}{10}$ $\frac{\square}{12}$

26. Estimate 15×34 by rounding each number to the nearest ten.

______

27. An angle represents $\frac{1}{6}$ of a circle. Use the numbers on the tiles to complete the equation and find the measure of the angle in degrees. Numbers may be used once, more than once, or not at all.

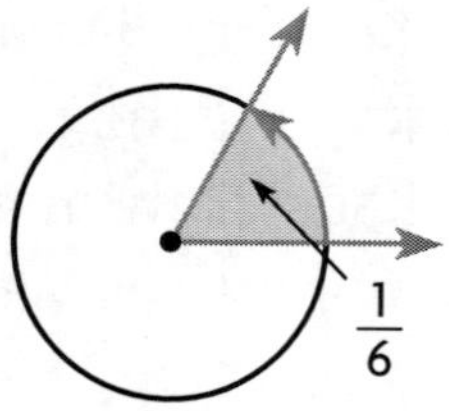

$\frac{1}{6} = \frac{1 \times \square}{6 \times \square} = \frac{\square}{360}$

50

60

64

The angle measure is ______.

28. Represent the shaded part of the fraction bar as the product of a whole number and a unit fraction.

$\frac{1}{12}$	$\frac{1}{12}$	$\frac{1}{12}$	$\frac{1}{12}$	$\frac{1}{12}$	$\frac{1}{12}$	$\frac{1}{12}$	$\frac{1}{12}$	$\frac{1}{12}$	$\frac{1}{12}$	$\frac{1}{12}$	$\frac{1}{12}$

29. Jimmy made $\frac{4}{5}$ gallon of lemonade for his friends. Jimmy's friends drank $\frac{2}{5}$ gallon of lemonade. How much lemonade is left?

$\square$ gallon

GO ON

Name ______________________________

Party Time!

Stefan and some friends organized a party for the people in his building. The party was held at a park across the street.

1. Mr. Hoya brought 5 watermelons from his grocery store. The watermelons weighed $8\frac{1}{4}$ pounds, $9\frac{1}{4}$ pounds, $8\frac{7}{8}$ pounds, $9\frac{5}{8}$ pounds, and $10\frac{3}{4}$ pounds. At the party, 153 people each ate a $\frac{1}{4}$-pound serving of watermelon. Was the amount of leftover watermelon less than, greater than, or equal to $8\frac{1}{2}$ pounds? Explain how to solve the problem. Then solve it.

____

____

____

____

____

The amount of watermelon leftover is _____ pounds.

2. Mr. Carlucci brought $8\frac{3}{4}$ pounds of turkey for large sandwiches. A skateboarder bumped into his table and $2\frac{7}{12}$ pounds of turkey fell to the ground. Mr. Carlucci wants to make 72 sandwiches with $\frac{1}{12}$ pound of turkey on each sandwich. Does he have enough turkey left to make his sandwiches? How much does he need or how much is left over? Show your work.

GO ON

3. The Salomans offered to be in charge of drinks for the party. In addition to other beverages, they brought 4 bags of coffee that each held $2\frac{1}{2}$ pounds. When brewed, $\frac{1}{4}$ pound of coffee made 8 cups of coffee. The Salomons brewed and served 296 cups of coffee. Was any coffee left over? If so, how much coffee was left? Show your work.

4. Ramone tossed 1 quarter, 2 dimes, and 13 pennies in the wishing well at the party. What is the total amount of money as a fraction and as a decimal? Show your work.

GO ON

Name ______________________________

5. At the party there were 380 places to sit, including the benches in the park and the chairs people brought to the party. Of those seats, 0.45 of them were used by women and girls. How many seats were used by men and boys? Is that fraction of the total number of seats less than or greater than $\frac{3}{5}$? Draw or use a visual fraction model if needed to solve.

____

____

____

6. Some of the neighbors played a penny game. Players tossed a penny in a hole and earned that number of points. Each player tossed 3 pennies. The scores from each penny that went in a hole were added for a final score. Was it possible to get a score of 9? If so, how could it have happened?

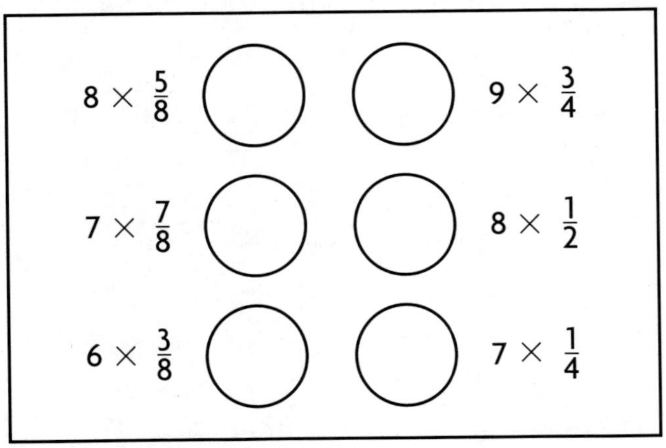

____

____

____

____

GO ON

7. Stefan and his friends used four tables for all the dishes the guests brought to the party. The tables were $2\frac{8}{10}$ meters long, 2.48 meters long, $2\frac{59}{100}$ meters long, and 2.84 meters long. Draw one way to model these numbers to compare them if needed to help solve. Write each as a decimal and order them from greatest to least using symbols.

8. One of the neighborhood apartment buildings has 8 floors, numbered 1 through 8. During the party, the elevator in the building was busy taking people up and down. The elevator started on the first floor. It went up $\frac{3}{8}$ of the building height, up another $\frac{2}{8}$ of the building, down $\frac{4}{8}$, up $\frac{6}{8}$, down $\frac{3}{8}$, and up $\frac{1}{8}$. What floor is the elevator on now? What move will put it back on the first floor?

____

____

____

____

STOP

Name ____________________

1. Kareem has 35 grapes that he is putting in 2 bowls. He wants to put the same number of grapes in each bowl. How many grapes will be in each bowl? Will there be any left over?

   There will be ________ grapes in each bowl with ________ left over.

2. Which quotients are equal to 200? Mark all that apply.

   Ⓐ $900 \div 3$

   Ⓑ $800 \div 4$

   Ⓒ $800 \div 2$

   Ⓓ $700 \div 6$

   Ⓔ $600 \div 3$

   Ⓕ $400 \div 2$

3. The town council has 10 members. Last year, 4 members ran for reelection. Write a fraction that is equivalent to $\frac{4}{10}$.

4. On opening night of the school play, there were 45 people in the audience. On the second night, 3 times as many people came to see the play. How many people came to see the play on the second night?

   ________ people

GO ON

Name ______________________________

5. For numbers 5a–5d, write the number that completes the equation.

5a. $35 \times 10 = \square$

5b. $19 \times \square = 380$

5c. $\square \times 100 = 1{,}200$

5d. $70 \times \square = 7{,}000$

6. Edgar, Jack, and Katie walked around Woodbury Lake. Edgar walked $\frac{3}{5}$ of the distance in an hour. Jack walked $\frac{3}{4}$ of the distance in an hour. Ellen walked $\frac{6}{8}$ of the distance in an hour. Compare the distances walked by each person by matching the statements to the correct symbol. Each symbol may be used once, more than once, or not at all.

$\frac{3}{5} \bigcirc \frac{3}{4}$ •	• $<$
$\frac{6}{8} \bigcirc \frac{3}{4}$ •	• $>$
$\frac{3}{5} \bigcirc \frac{6}{8}$ •	• $=$

7. James works in a flower shop and is putting tulips in vases for a wedding. He wants to put 7 tulips in each of 14 vases. He has 47 yellow tulips and 53 pink tulips.

James [does / does not] have enough tulips for the vases. He will have [0 / 2 / 3] tulips left over.

8. Sandi buys some fabric to make a quilt. She needs $\frac{1}{6}$ yard of each type of fabric. She has 7 different types of fabric to make her design. Write the number in the box to complete the equation.

$\frac{7}{6} = \square \times \frac{1}{6}$

GO ON

9. There are 122 fourth grade students and 11 teachers going on a field trip. Mrs. Reyes says they will need 8 busses for the trip. Each bus has room for 16 people.

Part A

Write a division equation that shows the total number of students and teachers going on the field trip divided among 8 busses. Then solve.

Part B

Is Mrs. Reyes correct that the students and teachers will need 8 busses? Explain your answer.

10. Draw place value models to show 1,534.

11. Royce walks $\frac{3}{4}$ mile to school and $\frac{3}{4}$ mile home each day.

In 2 days, Royce will walk [2 / 3 / 4] miles.

GO ON

12. Nina ran $\frac{2}{4}$ mile on Monday. She ran $\frac{3}{4}$ mile on Tuesday. How far did she run on Monday and Tuesday? Write an equation to help you solve.

13. The table shows the height of several mountains. Which statements are true? Mark all that apply.

U.S. Mountain Peaks					
Name	**State**	**Height (ft)**	**Name**	**State**	**Height (ft)**
Blanca Peak	CO	14,345	Mount Whitney	CA	14,494
Crestone Peak	CO	14,294	University Peak	AK	14,470
Humboldt Peak	CO	14,064	White Mountain	CA	14,246

Ⓐ Blanca Peak < Mount Whitney

Ⓑ Crestone Peak > University Peak

Ⓒ Humboldt Peak > Mount Whitney

Ⓓ Blanca Peak > White Mountain

14. Which numbers correctly complete the statements?

14a. 7,000 is 10 times [7,000 / 700 / 70 / 7].

14b. [6,000 / 600 / 60 / 6] is 10 times 60.

15. Margaret has 7 times as many pencils as Jake. Jake has 8 pencils. How many pencils does Margaret have?

________ pencils

GO ON

16. Write the unknown digits. Use each digit exactly once.

1	2	4	6	7

```
      4 5 8
  ×       9
  ---------
   3,☐ 0 0
     ☐ 5 0
  +    ☐ 2
  ---------
   4,☐ 2 ☐
```

17. Britney measures $\frac{7}{8}$ cup of milk for a recipe. Select a way $\frac{7}{8}$ can be written as a sum of fractions. Mark all that apply.

Ⓐ $\frac{1}{8} + \frac{1}{8} + \frac{1}{8} + \frac{1}{8} + \frac{1}{8} + \frac{1}{8} + \frac{1}{8}$

Ⓑ $\frac{2}{8} + \frac{2}{8} + \frac{1}{8}$

Ⓒ $\frac{2}{8} + \frac{2}{8} + \frac{1}{8} + \frac{1}{8} + \frac{1}{8}$

Ⓓ $\frac{4}{8} + \frac{4}{8}$

Ⓔ $\frac{3}{8} + \frac{2}{8} + \frac{2}{8}$

Ⓕ $\frac{1}{8} + \frac{1}{8} + \frac{2}{8} + \frac{3}{8}$

18. Rudi is comparing shark lengths. She read that a sandbar shark is $4\frac{1}{2}$ feet long. A thresher shark is 3 times as long as a sandbar shark. Find the length of a thresher shark.

A thresher shark is ________ feet long.

GO ON

19. Brett made this pictograph to show the number of points he scored in each game this month.

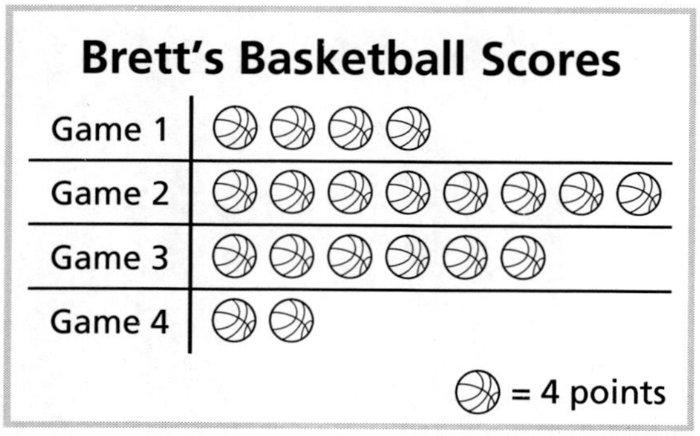

Part A

How many fewer points did Brett score in Game 1 than in Game 3? Write and solve an equation.

Equation: ______________

Answer: ______ fewer points

Part B

Choose the number that makes the sentence true.

Brett forgot to include Game 5 on his graph. He scored two times as many points in Game 5 as he scored in Game 4.

Brett scored [4 / 12 / 16 / 20] points in Game 5.

Part C

Explain how you determined the number of points Brett scored in Game 5.

GO ON

Name ______________________________

20. Fill in the numbers to find the sum.

$$\frac{4}{10} + \frac{\square}{10} = \frac{8}{\square}$$

21. Joe ran $\frac{5}{6}$ mile each day for 5 days. How far did Joe run? Write an equation and show your work. You may draw a fraction model to solve.

22. Write a related multiplication equation to help you solve.

$196 \div 4 =$ ______

______ $\times$ ______ $= 196$

23. Margie and Sam collect stamps. Margie has collected 4 times as many stamps as Sam. Together, they have 210 stamps. How many stamps does each person have? Show your work.

24. Draw a line to show the mixed number and expression that have the same value.

$1\frac{2}{5}$	$2\frac{3}{8}$	$4\frac{1}{3}$	$1\frac{2}{3}$
•	•	•	•
•	•	•	•
$\frac{2}{3} + \frac{1}{3} + \frac{1}{3}$	$1 + 1 + \frac{3}{3} + \frac{3}{3} + \frac{1}{3}$	$\frac{2}{3} + \frac{2}{3}$	$\frac{2}{5} + \frac{2}{5} + \frac{2}{5} + \frac{2}{5}$

GO ON

25. Which pairs of fractions are equivalent? Mark all that apply.

Ⓐ $\frac{8}{12}$ and $\frac{2}{3}$

Ⓑ $\frac{3}{4}$ and $\frac{10}{12}$

Ⓒ $\frac{4}{5}$ and $\frac{8}{12}$

Ⓓ $\frac{3}{5}$ and $\frac{60}{100}$

26. What is the product of 1,943 × 6? Show your work.

27. Janice ran $\frac{2}{5}$ mile on Tuesday. What is another way to write $\frac{2}{5}$? Use the numbers on the tiles to complete the equation. Numbers may be used once, more than once, or not at all.

$$\frac{2}{5} = \frac{2 \times \square}{5 \times \square} = \frac{\square}{100}$$

20
25
40

28. Complete the table to show the fraction as a product of a whole number and a unit fraction.

Fraction	Product
$\frac{2}{5}$	______
$\frac{7}{8}$	______
$\frac{4}{10}$	______

29. Shawnda ran $\frac{7}{12}$ mile on Monday and $\frac{3}{12}$ mile more than that on Tuesday. How far did Shawnda run on Tuesday?

__________ mile

GO ON

Name ______________________________

Middle-of-Year Performance Task

Building a House

Ben the Builder is building a house for the Johnson family. He needs to use his math skills to build the house correctly.

1. Ben multiplied the number of drywall screws he needs per room by the number of rooms in the house. He spilled water on the paper on which he was doing his calculations and some of the numbers are hard to read. Now his paper looks like this.

$$\begin{array}{r} 4{,}38\square \\ \times \qquad 5 \\ \hline \square 0{,}000 \\ 1{,}\square 00 \\ \square 00 \\ 30 \\ \hline 21{,}\square 30 \end{array}$$

What are the missing numbers? How many screws does Ben need? Show your work.

GO ON

2. Ben will hire a crane to help the workers put the bundles of shingles on the roof. There is a limit to the weight the crane can lift at one time, but Ben wants the work done as quickly as possible. Explain to Ben what math he can use so that the crane uses the fewest lifts possible.

____

____

____

3. Ben needs to choose between three brands of shingles to use on the roof. He knows he needs 89 bundles of shingles, but each type of shingle weighs a different amount. He needs to take the information he has about the cost of the crane and the amount it can lift to determine the cost of using each brand.

The crane costs \$350 plus an additional \$150 for each hour or part of an hour the crane is used. The crane can make 4 lifts in one hour. Each lift must weigh 650 pounds or less. The weights of a bundle of each brand of shingle can be found in the table below.

Complete the table. Show your work. Then decide which brand of shingles Ben should choose. Explain your reasoning.

Shingle	Weight of each Bundle (lb)	Number of Bundles in One Lift	Number of Lifts Needed	Number of Hours Needed	Total Cost of the Crane
Brand A	75				
Brand B	80				
Brand C	85				

GO ON

4. Ben wants to paint the inside of the house. The house has 2,100 square feet of wall to paint. Each gallon of paint can cover 350 square feet. Ben has 7 gallons of paint.

How many square feet can Ben cover with the paint he has? Show your work.

Ben can paint ______ square feet.

Does Ben have enough paint? How do you know?

____

____

5. Ben calculates that he needs 145 square feet of carpet for one room. The carpet store sells carpet by the square yard. There are 9 square feet in a yard. How many square yards of carpet does Ben need?

$145 \div 9 =$ ______

Ben needs ______ square yards of carpet.

GO ON

Name ____

6. This is the floor plan for the first floor of the house Ben is building.

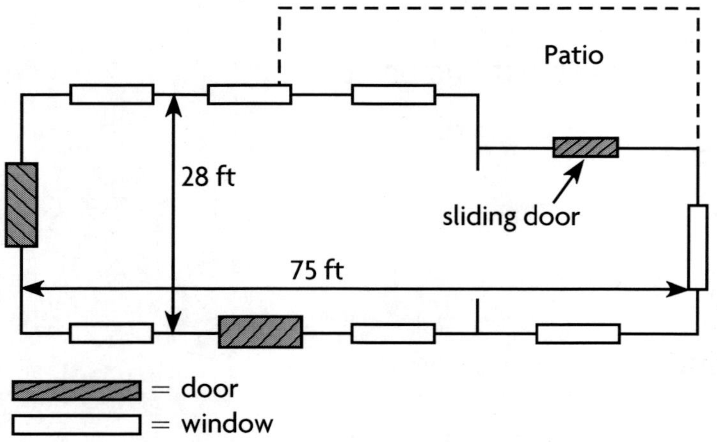

Ben needs to buy trim for around the windows and doors of the house. Complete the table to determine how much trim he should buy. Show your work.

Remember: Windows are trimmed on all four sides. Doors are not trimmed along the bottom.

Item	Number	Height (in.)	Width (in.)	Trim Needed (in.)
Window		48	40	
Door		80	36	
Sliding door		80	72	
			Total	

STOP

Name ______________________________

1. Lana bought party favors at a store for her school's 6th grade graduation party. She bought 7 bags of party hats with 12 hats in each bag. She also bought 4 bags of horns with 24 horns in each bag.

Part A

How many more horns than party hats did Lana buy? Show your work.

Part B

In addition to the party hats and horns, Lana also bought 3 bags of whistles with 18 whistles in each bag. When the party started, Lana found that 19 out of the total number of party favors were broken. How many of the party favors were unbroken?

______

2. How many acute angles does a right triangle have?

A right triangle has ______ acute angles.

3. Harrison rode his bike $\frac{6}{10}$ of a mile to the park. Shade the model. Then write $\frac{6}{10}$ as a decimal to show how far Harrison rode his bike.

Harrison rode his bike ______ mile to the park.

4. Use the rule to write the first five terms of the pattern.

Rule: Subtract 3, multiply by 2 First term: 8

____

GO ON

5. Select another way to show 25×18. Mark all that apply.

Ⓐ $(20 \times 10) + (20 \times 8) + (5 \times 10) + (5 \times 8)$

Ⓑ $(25 \times 20) + (25 \times 5) + (25 \times 10) + (25 \times 8)$

Ⓒ $(20 \times 18) + (5 \times 10) + (5 \times 8)$

Ⓓ $(25 \times 10) + (25 \times 8)$

Ⓔ $(25 \times 20) + (25 \times 5)$

6. Ann runs $\frac{2}{5}$ mile. Kim runs $\frac{3}{4}$ mile. They want to compare how far they each ran. Circle the symbol that completes the comparison.

$\frac{2}{5}$	$<$ $>$ $=$	$\frac{3}{4}$

7. Serena has several packages of raisins. Each package contains 3 boxes of raisins. Which could be the number of boxes of raisins Serena has? Mark all that apply.

Ⓐ 9 Ⓑ 18 Ⓒ 23 Ⓓ 27 Ⓔ 32

8. Phil made a number line showing the multiples of $\frac{3}{6}$.

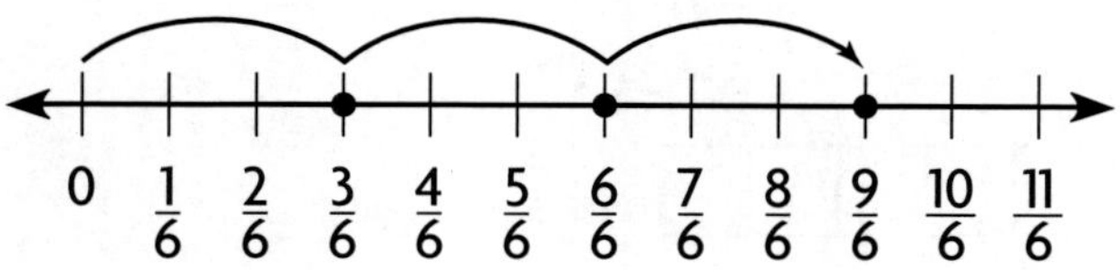

The product $2 \times \frac{3}{6}$ is shown by the fraction ________ on the number line.

GO ON

9. Determine whether each measurement is equivalent to 3 meters, 35 centimeters, or 300 millimeters. Write the measurement in the correct box.

3,000 millimeters	300 centimeters	30 centimeters
$\frac{35}{100}$ meter	0.300 meter	0.35 meter
$\frac{300}{1,000}$ meter	350 millimeters	30 decimeters

3 meters	35 centimeters	300 millimeters

10. Draw a place value model to show 4,362.

11. Three girls are selling cases of popcorn to earn money for a band trip. In their first week, Emily sold $2\frac{3}{4}$ cases, Brenda sold $4\frac{1}{4}$ cases, and Shannon sold $3\frac{1}{2}$ cases.

Part A

How many cases of popcorn have the girls sold in all?

Part B

The girls must sell a total of 35 cases in order to have enough money for the trip. Suppose they sell the same amount in each of the following 2 weeks as they sold in the first week. Will the girls have sold enough cases of popcorn to go on the trip? Explain.

GO ON

Name ____

12. A circle is divided into parts. Which sum could represent the angle measures that make up the circle? Mark all that apply.

Ⓐ 120° + 120° + 120°

Ⓑ 47° + 61° + 78° + 83° + 101°

Ⓒ 15° + 40° + 53° + 62° + 90° + 100°

Ⓓ 20° + 30° + 60° + 70°

13.

Mountain Peaks of Canada			
Name	**Height (ft)**	**Name**	**Height (ft)**
Centennial Peak	12,533	Mount Root	12,799
Mount Columbia	12,293	Mount Tiedemann	12,625
Mount King George	12,274	North Twin	12,247

Write the name of each mountain in the box that describes its height, in feet.

Between 12,240 feet and 12,500 feet	Between 12,501 feet and 12,800 feet

14. Kelly has 236 feet of fencing material to use to enclose a rectangular space for her dog. She wants to use all of the fencing material. She also wants the width to be 23 feet. Draw a rectangle that could be the space for Kelly's dog. Label the length and the width.

15. Write the letter for each figure below the correct number of lines of symmetry it has.

A B C D

0 lines of symmetry	**1 line of symmetry**	**2 lines of symmetry**	**More than 2 lines of symmetry**
☐	☐	☐	☐

GO ON

Name ______________________

16. A total of 5,437 visitors went to a theme park on Monday and Tuesday. If 3,758 visitors went to the theme park on Monday, how many visitors went to the park on Tuesday? Show your work.

17. Write the word that describes the part of Figure A written below.

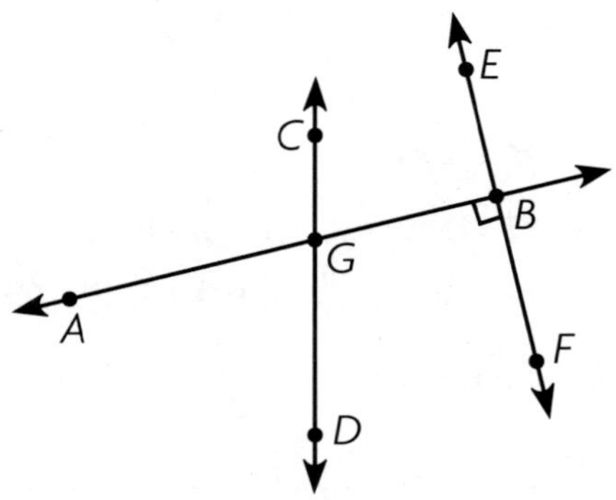

Figure A

ray	line	line segment	acute angle	right angle

$\overline{AG}$ ______________

$\overleftrightarrow{EF}$ ______________

$\overrightarrow{GC}$ ______________

$\angle GBF$ ______________

$\angle AGD$ ______________

18. Trevor's pet goat weighed $6\frac{3}{8}$ pounds when it was born. By age 3, the goat weighed 8 times as much. Use the numbers and symbols on the tiles to show how to find the weight of Trevor's goat at age 3. Not all numbers and symbols will be used.

$8\frac{3}{8}$	8	3
$6\frac{3}{8}$	$+$	$\times$

weight = ☐ ☐ ☐

GO ON

19. Charlotte made this pictograph to show the number of dogs attending a dog training class this week.

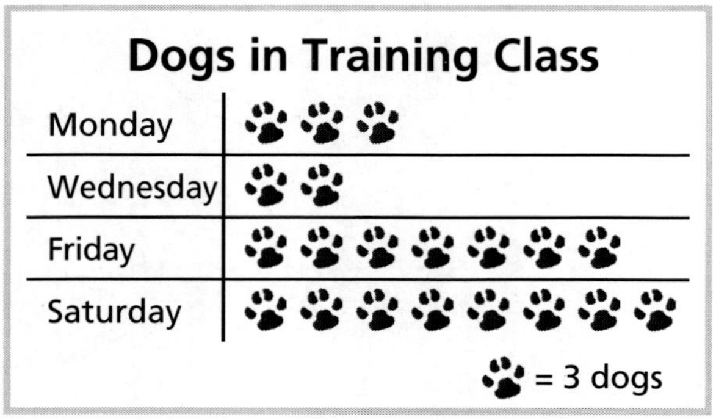

Part A

How many fewer dogs were in training class on Monday than on Friday? Write and solve an equation.

Equation: ______________

Answer: ______________ fewer dogs

Part B

Choose the number that makes the sentence true.

Charlotte forgot to include Thursday on her graph. There were two times as many dogs at Thursday's class as there were at Monday's class.

There were [2 / 6 / 15 / 18] dogs in the training class on Thursday.

20. Fill in the numbers to find the sum.

$$\frac{2}{10} + \frac{\square}{100} = \frac{5}{\square}$$

GO ON

Name ______________________________

21. The table shows how many liters of water people drank during a picnic. Complete the line plot to show the data.

Amount of Water Consumed (in liters)
$\frac{1}{7}, \frac{3}{7}, \frac{3}{7}, \frac{2}{7}, \frac{1}{7}, \frac{2}{7}, \frac{1}{7}, \frac{5}{7}$

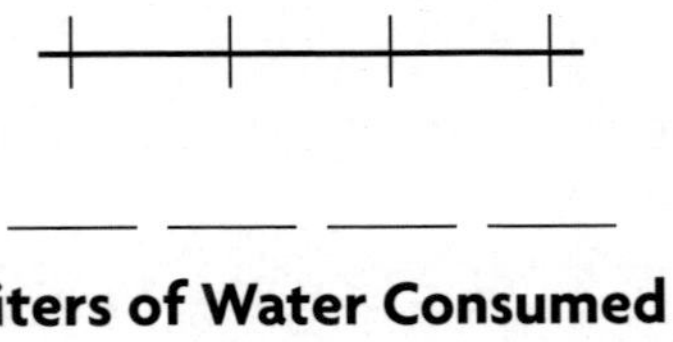

22. An author signed books at a book store starting at 11:00 A.M. She signed books for 1 hour 25 minutes. Draw jumps on the time line to determine the end time.

The author stopped signing books at ________ P.M.

23. Jane and Marcus both create place mats out of lace trim. Marcus uses 3 times as much lace as Jane. Together, they use 64 inches of lace trim making place mats. How much lace does each person use? Write an equation and solve.

24. Ellie's mom sells toys. She sold $\frac{7}{10}$ of the toys. Select a way $\frac{7}{10}$ can be written as a sum of fractions. Mark all that apply.

Ⓐ $\frac{4}{10} + \frac{1}{10} + \frac{1}{10} + \frac{1}{10}$

Ⓑ $\frac{4}{10} + \frac{3}{10} + \frac{1}{10} + \frac{1}{10} + \frac{1}{10}$

Ⓒ $\frac{1}{10} + \frac{2}{10} + \frac{3}{10} + \frac{1}{10}$

GO ON

25. Which pairs of fractions are equivalent? Mark all that apply.

Ⓐ $\frac{4}{5}$ and $\frac{6}{8}$

Ⓑ $\frac{2}{6}$ and $\frac{1}{3}$

Ⓒ $\frac{2}{3}$ and $\frac{8}{12}$

Ⓓ $\frac{1}{4}$ and $\frac{2}{10}$

26. Circle the number in the box that best completes the statement.

The product of 39 and 122 is closest to [3,000 / 4,000 / 4,800 / 5,200].

27. An angle represents $\frac{1}{20}$ of a circle. Use the numbers on the tiles to show how to find the measure of the angle in degrees. Numbers may be used once, more than once, or not at all.

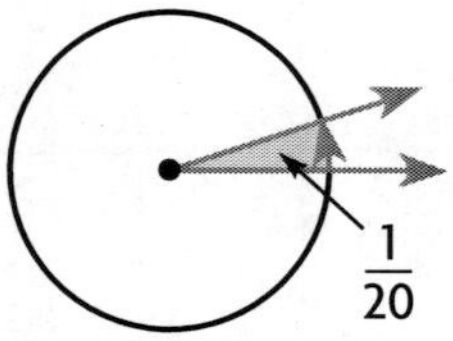

$$\frac{1}{20} = \frac{1 \times \square}{20 \times \square} = \frac{\square}{360}$$

The angle measure is ______.

14

18

36

28. Represent the shaded part of the fraction bar as the product of a whole number and a unit fraction.

$\frac{1}{10}$	$\frac{1}{10}$	$\frac{1}{10}$	$\frac{1}{10}$	$\frac{1}{10}$	$\frac{1}{10}$	$\frac{1}{10}$	$\frac{1}{10}$	$\frac{1}{10}$	$\frac{1}{10}$

29. Eric made $\frac{7}{8}$ cup of trail mix. He ate $\frac{1}{8}$ cup of trail mix. How much trail mix does Eric have left?

☐ cup

GO ON

Name ______________________________

End-of-Year
Performance Task

Talking Trash

1. An office building has a cement pad under its dumpster. The pad has an area of 108 square feet. The dumpster is 9 feet long and 8 feet wide. What is the most likely perimeter of the cement pad?

2. A garbage collection service uses this design to identify its trucks.

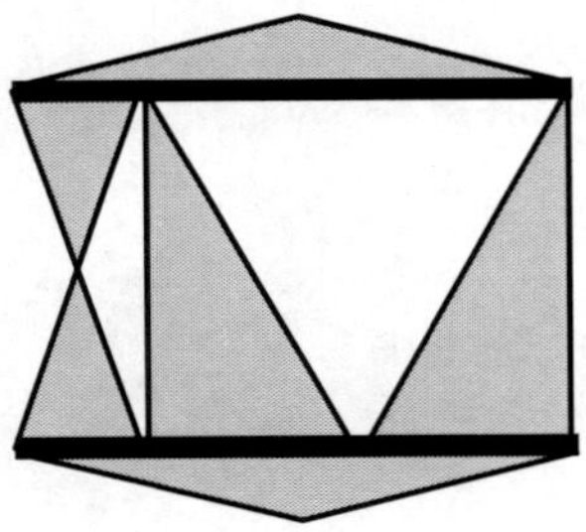

Name each kind of shaded triangle in the design.

____

____

____

GO ON

Name ________________________

3. A competing garbage collection service, *I Canned It!*, is making a new design. The shape below shows what has been designed so far.

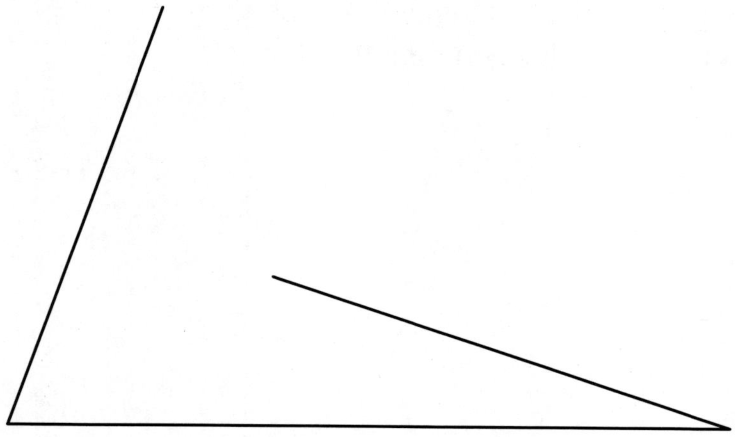

a. Use a protractor to measure each angle. Write the measurements.

____

b. Complete the design. Add at least 2 more angles of 45° and 120° to the drawing. Record all angle measurements.

GO ON

Name ______________________

4. This sketch shows the area where one of ABC Garbage Collection's trucks picks up trash on Tuesdays and Fridays.

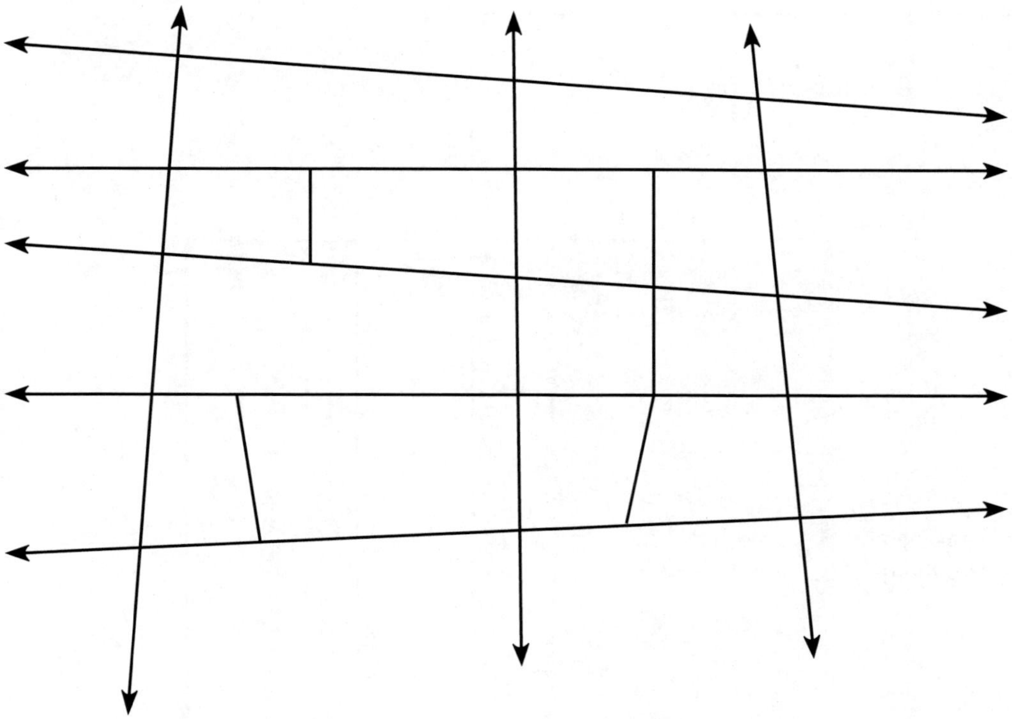

a. Label a pair of parallel lines, a pair of perpendicular lines, and a line segment in the sketch. List them in the spaces below.

parallel lines ______________________

perpendicular lines ______________________

line segment ______________________

b. Is there a quadrilateral formed by the sketch? If so, what is its name? Explain your mathematical thinking.

____

____

____

____

GO ON

Name ____________________

5. The parking lots at *We Dump It* trash collection service are divided up into sections for loading and unloading, truck parking, and employee parking.

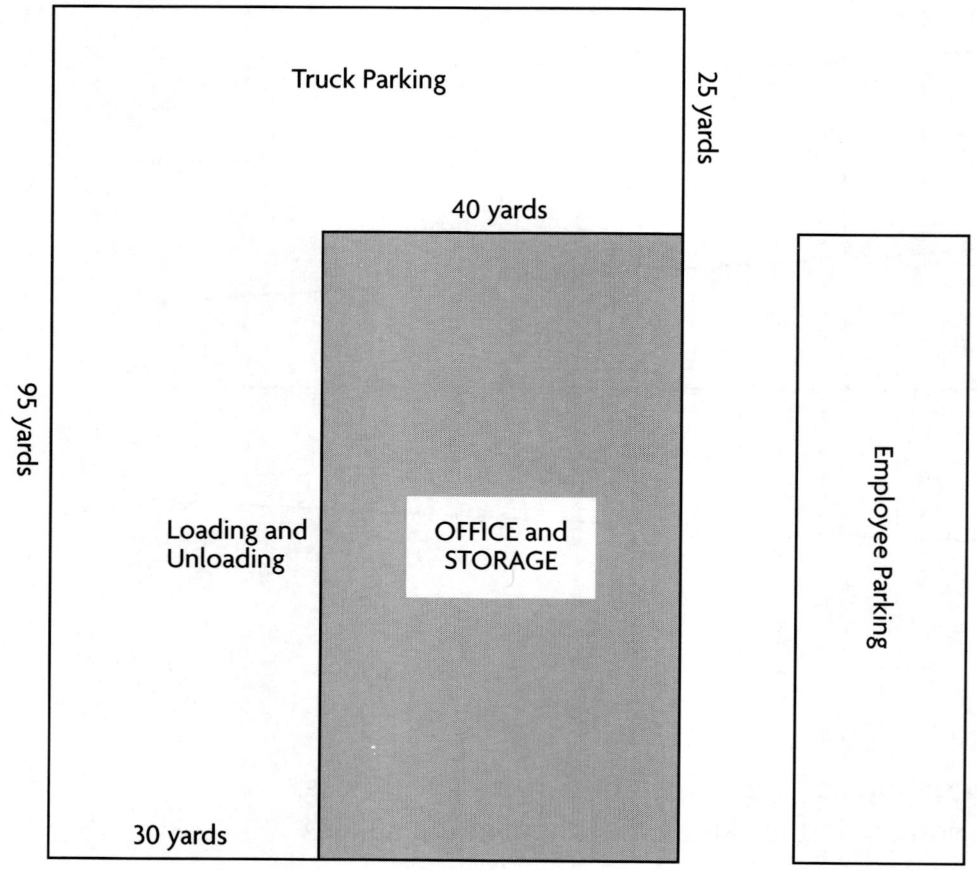

a. The Employee Parking lot has an area of 378 square yards. The parking lot is 9 yards wide. What is the perimeter of the Employee Parking lot?

____

b. What is the area of the Loading and Unloading and the Truck Parking lots combined? Explain your mathematical thinking.

____

____

____

____

____

STOP

Name ______________________________

Musical Madness

Mr. Barnes, the theater teacher at LaMonte Elementary School, is planning for the annual spring musical. He took a survey to find out how many students in each grade would most like to act, sing, or dance. This chart represents his findings:

	Act	Sing	Dance
Grade 1	14	25	17
Grade 2	7	12	39
Grade 3	23	9	15
Grade 4	12	19	5
Grade 5	15	20	22

Mr. Barnes also wanted to know how many students would be interested in helping backstage with lights, sound, and costumes. He wrote down the number of interested students in each grade, but he lost the information. He remembers that in first grade, 20 students were interested. Twice as many students were interested in second grade. Third and fourth grade had the same number of interested students, but the number was 5 less than in second grade. The number of interested students in fourth grade was 5 times the number of interested students in fifth grade.

20	______	______	______	______
Grade 1	Grade 2	Grade 3	Grade 4	Grade 5

GO ON

Name ________________________________

The art teacher, Mrs. Keys, agrees to help with costumes. Most of the costumes can be found in storage, but she wants to supplement what's available with extra fabric. Mrs. Keys says that for Grades 1–3, she will need $\frac{1}{8}$ yard of purple fabric for every singer, $\frac{1}{6}$ yard of black fabric for every actor, and $\frac{1}{2}$ yard of blue fabric for every dancer. For the singers, dancers, and actors in Grades 4–5, she will need twice as much fabric as she needs for the singers, dancers, and actors in Grades 1–3.

The shop teacher, Ms. McKay, tells Mr. Barnes she will be happy to help hang the curtains. The very tall curtains that hang from the ceiling to the floor are folded up in boxes in storage. The curtains have been folded in half top to bottom once and then in half from top to bottom again. While folded, the curtains measure 4 ft tall.

When the play is ready to be performed, Mr. Barnes, Mrs. Keys, and Ms. McKay set up chairs in the auditorium. The audience has three sections, labeled on the diagram as A, B, and C.

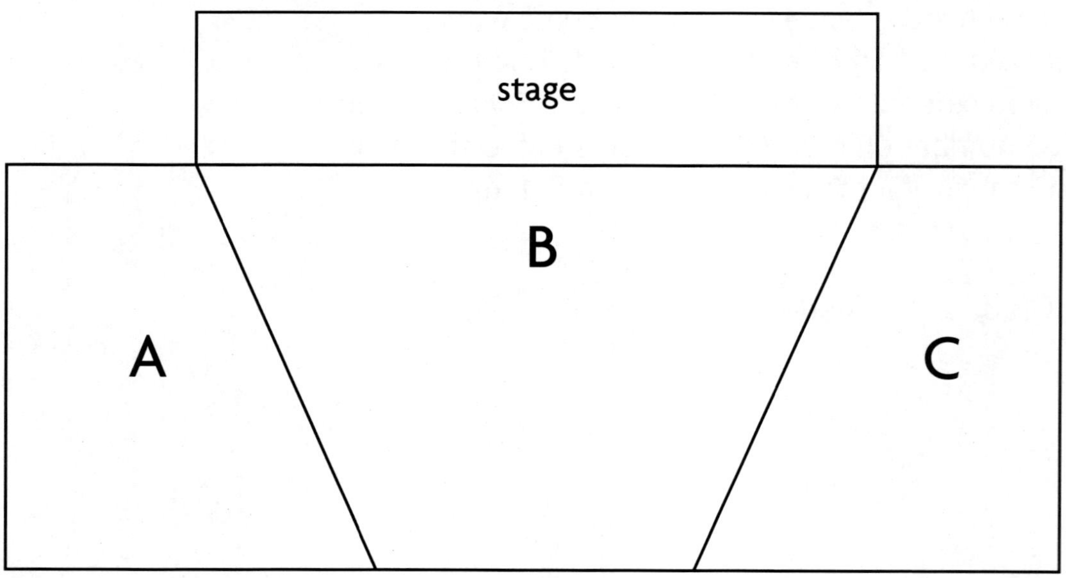

GO ON

Name ______________________________

1. Determine how many students in each grade have an interest in working backstage.

20	______	______	______	______
Grade 1	Grade 2	Grade 3	Grade 4	Grade 5

2a. If each of the 254 students who perform on stage has 3 friends come to see the musical, and each of the 137 students working back stage has 2 friends come to see the musical, how many total audience members will there be?

There will be ____________ audience members.

2b. If sections A and C can both fit 30 rows of 9 chairs, and section B can fit 32 rows of 24 chairs, will there be enough chairs for all the audience members? If not, how many more are needed? If so, how many will be left over?

There are ____________ chairs in section A.

There are ____________ chairs in section B.

There are ____________ chairs in section C.

There are ____________ total chairs.

GO ON

3. The musical the students are performing contains 9 songs.

a. If Mr. Barnes wants 10 students to sing each song, how many students will get to sing more than 1 song? Explain your answer.

____

____

____

____

b. Mr. Barnes also wants the same number of dancers to dance for each song. How many dancers can he have for each song without leaving anyone out? How many dancers will need to dance more than one song to make this happen? Explain your answer.

____

____

____

____

____

____

c. Mr. Barnes has a scene to be performed by 5 actors. He wants the scene to be performed by actors in the same grade, but he doesn't want anyone to act twice. Which grade can perform the scene, and how many times will the scene be performed so that everyone can have a chance to perform?

____

____

____

____

____

GO ON

Name ______________________

4. Complete the chart showing how many yards of fabric Mrs. Keys needs for each student in Grades 1–3 and in Grades 4–5.

Fabric (in yards)			
	Black Fabric	Purple Fabric	Blue Fabric
Grades 1–3	$\frac{1}{6}$	$\frac{1}{8}$	$\frac{1}{2}$
Grades 4–5			

5. Expand the chart to include the number of students in each category. Use the chart to help you calculate the total number of yards of each color of fabric Mrs. Keys needs. Write the answer in order from greatest to least.

	Actors	Black Fabric	Total	Singers	Purple Fabric	Total	Dancers	Blue Fabric	Total
G 1–3		$\frac{1}{6}$			$\frac{1}{8}$			$\frac{1}{2}$	
G 4–5									

____

____

____

Mrs. Keys needs ________ yards of ________ fabric, ________ yards of ________ fabric, and ________ yards of ________ fabric.

GO ON

6. The figure below represents the curtains in storage. Draw dotted lines to represent what the fabric will look like when it's unfolded. Then, calculate the height of the curtains.

4 ft

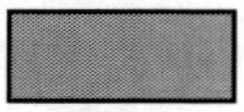

The height of the curtain is ________ feet.

7. Mr. Barnes explains to the students in the musical that every stage has imaginary lines drawn on it. The first imaginary line of symmetry runs up and down and separates the stage into halves called "stage right" and "stage left." Stage right refers to the right side of stage from the perspective of the actor who is standing on stage and facing the audience. The second imaginary line of symmetry runs side to side and separates the stage into two halves called "upstage" and "downstage." Upstage refers to the part of the stage farthest away from the audience, and downstage refers to the part of the stage closest to the audience.

a. Draw the imaginary vertical line of symmetry to separate the stage and label the parts "stage right" and "stage left."

b. Draw the imaginary horizontal line of symmetry to separate the stage into symmetrical parts and label those parts "upstage" and "downstage."

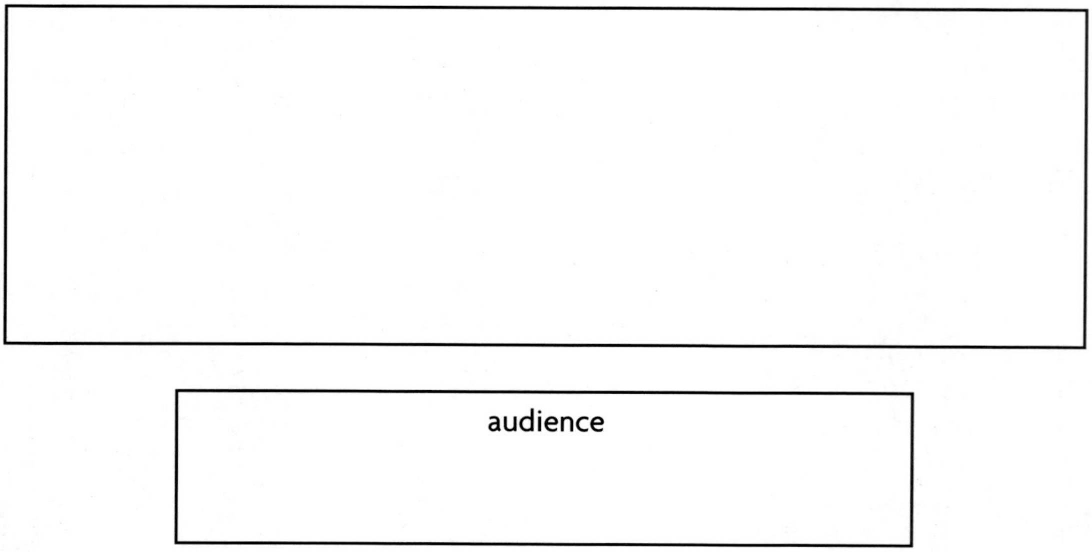

STOP